CD-ROM for Librarians and Educators

CD-ROM
for Librarians
and Educators

A Resource Guide to
Over 300 Instructional Programs

by
BARBARA HEAD SORROW
and
BETTY S. LUMPKIN

McFarland & Company, Inc., Publishers
Jefferson, North Carolina, and London

British Library Cataloguing-in-Publication data are available

Library of Congress Cataloguing-in-Publication Data

Sorrow, Barbara.
    CD-ROM for librarians and educators : a resource guide to over 300
instructional programs / by Barbara Head Sorrow and Betty S.
Lumpkin.
      p. cm.
    Includes bibliographical references and index.
    ISBN 0-89950-800-6 (sewn softcover : 55# alk. paper) ∞
    1. Computer-assisted instruction—United States—Software—
Catalogs. 2. Computer-assisted instruction—United States—
Computer programs—Catalogs. 3. Data bases—United States—
Catalogs. 4. CD-ROM—United States—Catalogs. 5. CD-ROM industry—
United States—Directories. 6. School libraries—United States—
Book lists. I. Lumpkin, Betty S., 1934— . II. Title.
LB1028.7.S67 1993
371.3′34′0216—dc20   92-56700
                                                      CIP

Manufactured in the United States of America

McFarland & Company, Inc., Publishers
  Box 611, Jefferson, North Carolina 28640

Contents

Preface

The purpose of *CD-ROM for Librarians and Educators* is to present a dependable and useful annotated collection of CD-ROM resources which will benefit educators, librarians, counselors, students and parents. It provides evaluative criteria and lesson plans for the instructor and also acquaints the librarian and educator with a comprehensive range of distributors, producers, and resources.

The titles used in this guide are selected because of their versatility and ability to enhance the instructional process in the classroom or for independent individualized learning. This CD-ROM library is for kindergarten through college and is primarily devoted to specific subjects such as science, English, and foreign languages, and specific documentary forms such as citations found in indexes. However, there is a wealth of information on consumer goods, travel, current affairs, and general topics.

Teachers may use this guide to locate information that will enhance specific teaching strategies in the classroom. The librarian can use this handbook as a selection tool for building a collection and setting up work stations for students. Various strategies are provided which show the most productive ways of introducing CD-ROM to the educator and student.

One of the criteria the authors of this handbook used in selecting the titles was that the information be pertinent to students' growth. The producers and distributors are reliable and have proven dependable in their subject fields. Each entry has been carefully reviewed for objectivity, appeal to students, educational content, timeliness, format, and factual credibility.

Surveys, interviews, and previews were used to obtain information about the resources available to students in schools and colleges. The surveys and previews were analyzed thoroughly, and interviews were conducted with many librarians and educators about the desirability and credibility of specific materials proposed as instructional resources.

Each entry uses the following format:

Title: Name of CD-ROM program
Producer: Originator of the program
Format: Operating system
Subject: Academic field
Price: Catalog price
Grade level: Kindergarten through college, or
       general audience
Hardware: Hardware needed to run program
Software: Special software needed
Distributor: Contact for purchase
Description: Review of program

Information and access to information are crucial elements to societal progress in the United States. The right to electronic information has made educators and librarians respond to the critical process of selecting electronic information.

This handbook will benefit educators, as well as the general public, on the utilization of CD-ROM resources. Questions which many educators and students are asking have been discussed and methods of instruction have been made available.

ONE

CD-ROM Basics

Educators such as librarians, counselors, and teachers have been among the first to recognize the importance of technology in satisfying current information needs. Today, this multimedia technology is refining the instructional process of education, promoting the American Library Association's recognition of "information literate" people as those who are prepared to manipulate their environment and "learn how to learn."

CD-ROM is part of this exciting technology, which allows for the instant processing of information, enhancing all styles of learning. Some of the specific learning styles which students are bringing to the classroom are visual, informal, manipulative, dyadic, mobile, auditory, and haptic.

The haptic learner is the student who learns best when he or she is involved with moving, experimenting, and creating. The right brain characteristics are involved in this learning style.

The auditory learning style is when the student processes information that is heard, as through a lecture format. This is the traditional method of instruction in secondary schools or college. The student may benefit from teleconference education or long-distance learning. This may be one of the easiest methods of learning.

The visual learner demonstrates a preference for seeing the information. They may rely on pictures, visual aids, lists or graphs and can learn best with their classroom notes. This learner reads for information and usually does well on SAT tests or any standardized test because of reading ability.

The dyadic learners learn best with a small group or partner. Parents can help these students or can consider tutors if they are not achieving at their ability level.

The mobile learner needs to move around and take breaks from studying or frustration can become a factor. A traditional classroom setting where the child has to sit all day may not be a wise choice for this learner.

The informal reader is one who works better with the radio on or studying on the floor. The traditional desk and chair without any noise may not work for this student.

Other learning styles may be called by different names but may mean the same thing. For example, the analytic learner is similar to the auditory learner, already described. This learner also likes class lectures and taking notes. Thinking logically and evaluating the facts is important to this learner. Another style is called imaginative learner and is similar to the haptic style described above. This learner enjoys creative writing and tries to find out why information is important to him.

CD-ROM instructional technology is helping educators and parents address all learning styles and promote individualized instruction. The student is involved with his learning. CD-ROM is a storage device that uses laser technology to put data onto a compact disc. Each disc has an enormous storage capacity, about 250,000 pages of text. Since the data cannot be tampered with, this storage medium is ideal for library use: databases, textbooks, encyclopedias, etc. Bibliographic databases are fast finding acceptance in libraries. The Library of Congress is using CD-ROM to record everything that is in the card catalog. The great value is that CD-ROM holds a tremendous amount of information that is easily assessible.

According to EBSCO Publishing, CD-ROM has actually grown out of the very successful audio CD business. CD-ROM is the brainchild of Philips and Sony, the same companies that brought audio CD to the forefront of the music industry. CD-ROM uses the same technology that allows audiophiles to listen to over one hour of extremely high quality sound recorded on a plastic compact disc. On a CD-ROM disc, over 700 million characters of data can be stored — that's the equivalent of nearly 2,000 floppy disks or of the text in six sets of encyclopedias.

The clear advantage of CD-ROM as a medium for delivering information is that both the discs and the players can be mass produced quickly and economically. Add this to the tremendous amount of information that can be stored on such a small surface and you have all the key elements of a winning technology.

So what does this mean for the educational community? It means a further increase in the vast information available to the student. But it also means this information is far more readily accessible than it ever has been. CD-ROM has generated more excitement in the field of library science than any other technology since printing, with many librarians testifying that this is the solution to many of their information-handling problems. This certainly carries over to the education market because of the easy access for students.

Once information is located on the disc it is downloaded into the computer with the help of a CD-ROM disc drive or player. The information taken from the disc can now be manipulated and combined with other material from the hard disk and then sent to the printer.

Oliver Pesch, technical director for EBSCO Publishing, indicates that now CD-ROM has been with us for a few years, more and more libraries are turning their attention to the networking of CD-ROMs. By adding a "CD-ROM server" to a local area network, workstations on the network are able to access any database on the CD-ROM server, and, yes, more than one person can access the same information at the same time. The advantages to this advance in technology are both cost savings as well as improved access to information.

Whether you have a single workstation or a large network, for the educator and librarian the silver disc means more information in less space for less money with more permanency and ease of access.

Networking solves many of the problems a reference staff encounters when dealing with CD-ROM products. The staff is usually concerned with: keeping track of who has which CD-ROM database; CD-ROM discs becoming lost or damaged; damage to equipment resulting from improper handling; and the uneven demand of databases and workstations.

With a CD-ROM network, all of a library's databases can be mounted on a CD-ROM server located away from the public area. Each workstation has a network interface card installed in it and is connected to the CD-ROM server via coax cable. Running on each workstation is a menu system listing all of the databases available. Patrons can walk into the library, locate the first available workstation and select the desired database from the menu. It doesn't matter if one, two or even ten other people are using the same database. The CD-ROM network maximizes the use of the library's resources.

An added benefit to the network is that reference librarians do not have to worry about circulating CD-ROM discs. And because the CD-ROM discs are permanently mounted in the CD-ROM server (which would be secured), they cannot go astray or become damaged.

Typically a CD-ROM network provides librarians with the ability to place their CD-ROM databases in the CD-ROM players attached to one computer on their local area network and have all other workstations on the network access these CD-ROMs. A CD-ROM network is as effective for libraries with three or four workstations as it is for institutions with dozens of computers on their local area network. Multiple CD-ROM servers can be installed, with each one able to accommodate up to 32 CD-ROM players. The result is that literally hundreds of CD-ROM databases can be accessed from a single workstation.

Special software is needed to network CD-ROM data because network operating systems, such as Novell, do not provide such facilities. While the sharing of CD-ROM data is a prerequisite for any CD-ROM networking package, a few provide additional valuable features that help with the installation, operation, and maintenance of the network.

There are several important features that you should expect to find in a full-featured CD-ROM network: the CD-ROM network should be able to run any database that is compatible with Microsoft MS-DOS CD-ROM or MAC Extensions TM; two or more users must be able to search the same database at the same time as well as search different databases; an easy-to-maintain menu system will provide single keystroke access to any database mounted on the CD-ROM server.

Statistics kept on which databases are accessed and for what period of time will aid the library staff in seeing which ones are being used and which are not. This feature is valuable in helping with budget decisions and for planning future growth of the network.

Users should be prevented from accessing the C:/> prompt in order to eliminate problems that can occur when files are deleted or modified (inadvertently or otherwise). Additional security is provided if the CD-ROMs are mounted in the CD-ROM server and kept away from the public area.

The ability to limit the number of simultaneous users for a given copy of a database is another important feature that allows the library to enforce license agreements on products where such limits are imposed.

On busy networks, mounting multiple copies of popular databases can effectively balance the load and improve performance. Some networks allow multiple copies of a database to be mounted on the same CD-ROM servers or on different CD-ROM servers. The process of choosing the copy to use should be automatic and apparent to the user.

Even though the CD-ROM server can accommodate many CD-ROM databases, the workstation should only have to "open" the database being searched. This minimizes the amount of RAM required by Microsoft Extensions. (Note: the menu system can perform the "open" automatically when a user selects a database.)

Data is placed into memory as it is read from the CD-ROM disc in the server. A subsequent request for the same data is processed at memory speed, improving the performance of the network.

A good CD-ROM network will allow remote users, with modems connected to the PCs or dumb terminals, to access databases on the network through phone lines. (Note: additional hardware and software is generally required.)

One of the most common requests is to provide a way to have a CD-ROM application return to the menu when a user leaves the workstation and to assign one key that can be used to exit any CD-ROM product. These features enhance the user friendliness of the network.

On networks which use the workstations' hard disks to store the retrieval software, the process of installing a new product or revising new software can be time consuming. A utility (currently only available on EBSCO's CD-ROM Network) to automatically distribute the software simplifies this maintenance aspect of the network and ensures that all workstations are using the most current software.

While customer support may not be considered a feature by some, the ability to pick up a phone and get a knowledgeable person on the other end to help with problems is very important and should not be overlooked in evaluating a CD-ROM network solution.

Also coupled with customer service is the maintainability of the CD-ROM server. If one component of the server fails, is the entire network out of commission? If possible, the CD-ROM network vendor should provide the capability to set up a temporary server in such situations.

The availability of a CD-ROM network that improves the CD-ROM resources in a library is evidenced by the ever growing number of CD-ROM network installations. While the prospect of selecting and installing a CD-ROM network may seem somewhat daunting, be assured that effective solutions are available. Here is a list of ways networking can benefit the educational community: (1) Serve all students and library users; (2) Provide access to greater number of resources, materials, and human resources; (3) Cooperative effort to improve library system; (4) Joint meetings; (5) Open the lines of communication for a wider audience; (6) Form an area-wide organization of librarians and educators; (7) Allow for exchange of bibliographic materials; (8) Purchase materials cooperatively; (9) Jointly produce programs using all types of educational technology; (10) Interlibrary loan; (11) Cooperation between community colleges and schools; (12) Cooperative examination center; (13) Develop a joint community resource file; (14)Brainstorming opportunities to generate ideas for improving education; (15) Develop better communication.

LCD Panel

The LCD (liquid crystal display) projection panel projects computer-generated images onto a screen or wall using a transmissive overhead projector. No special software is required. Graphics and text from any software program can be displayed.

Most projection panels can be used with IBM PC or compatible, IBM PS/2, Apple Macintosh, and Apple II computers. An interface cable which fits the personal computer is required to adapt the panel to the computer. In some instances, video adapters may be required. Consult a dealer on specific requirements.

The LCD panels are compact and portable with dimensions of approximately 14″ w. × 14″ h. × 2.75″ d. and weight of about seven pounds. The power transformer weighs about two pounds. Some models offer carrying cases as optional accessories.

Projection panels are available in monochrome or various numbers of color displays. Some models are capable of displaying more than 226,000 colors! Price is determined by color display capabilities and features.

It is advisable to determine what the needs of the user are before deciding on the model. It is unwise to invest in a model with features which are not needed or to fail to obtain capabilities which might be essential to maximum use. If moving video and or animation capabilities are desired, the Lanier 4320V is an excellent panel. It is a high-resolution, true-color panel for large screen viewing of computer-based images and videos. It can project more than 226,000 vivid colors. It weighs less than six pounds and is compatible with popular personal computers.

This active-matrix LCD and video capabilities allow presenters to include video images or animations in their presentations. It is also possible with this model to watch videotapes from a VCR on a large screen.

The 4320V model is the high end of Lanier's LCD panel line. It offers a complete interactive presentation system, incorporating video, animation in full motion, audio capabilities, and high color fidelity.

Less expensive models are available and should be considered according to the needs of the user. If projection of moving video and animation is not a requirement, other models might fulfil the needs of the presenter at a much lower cost. It is highly recommended that before a purchase is made, several LCD panel models be investigated to determine which fits the needs of the user most adequately.

Depending on the area of the country, it might be difficult to find dealers who are knowledgeable about LCD panels and their use. One particularly helpful and informed dealer is Lanier Worldwide, Inc. (1-800-879-4002) with Karen Burns, Account Executive, as a representative who is well-versed in the LCD panel technology and willing to help with needs assessment.

To maximize the capabilities of the LCD panel, choose a transmissive overhead projector with uniform light intensity on the overhead projection platen. Also, select a projector which does not produce excessive amounts of heat. Consult an audio visual dealer to assist in determining the best overhead for satisfactory images.

The addition of a projection panel to the computer system is valuable in a classroom setting because it allows all students to see the same thing at the same time. To further enhance a classroom presentation, it is recommended that external speakers be added when the computer program includes sound. It is very impressive for instance, when a teacher is using a program such as *National Geographic's Mammals* to see the mammals moving across the screen and to hear the actual sounds of the mammals concurrently; or when using the *Grolier's Electronic Encyclopedia* to *see* such historical events as Kennedy's Inaugural Address or Dr. Martin Luther King's "I Have a Dream" speech and hear the text spoken in the actual voice of the historical figure. History then truly comes *alive*!

According to Sayett Technology, Inc., producer of LCD panels, some basic terms you need to know as you investigate and use LCD projection panels are:

pixel One dot or point in a CRT screen image. A CRT screen image is made up of a matrix of dots or points.

analog RGB video A video display system that uses an analog signal for each of the primary colors (red, green and blue) and translates each signal into a wide range of corresponding color intensities.

digital RGB video A video display system that uses a digital signal for each of the primary colors (red, green or blue). The signal determines if the color is on or off.

MDA IBM monochrome display adapter or a 100 percent compatible card (digital monochrome).

HGC Hercules graphics card or a 100 percent compatible graphics card (digital monochrome).

CGA IBM color/graphics adapter or a 100 percent compatible graphics card (digital RGB).

EGA IBM enhanced graphics adapter or 100 percent compatible graphics card (digital RGB).

MCGA IBM multi-color graphics array (analog RGB) or 100 percent compatible card. Refers to the integrated video subsystem in the IBM PS/2, models 25 and 30.

VGA IBM video graphics array (analog RGB) or 100 percent compatible card. Refers to the integrated video subsystem in the IBM PS/2, models 50, 60, and 80. The VGA is capable of higher display resolutions

(720×400 in text modes, 640×480 in graphics models). The VGA cards (and compatibles) are also available for use in the family of IBM PC or compatible computers.

transmissive overhead An overhead projector whose light source is below the object projected.

Workstations

The CD-ROM workstations are usually located in the reference area of the library allowing the user quick access to other reference materials and a reference librarian. Student population, academic and special education needs, teacher expertise, technical support, finances, and space are to be considered during initial planning for this technology.

Space is usually the most crucial consideration because a school is rarely able to purchase the needed electronic technology during the initial purchase. Educators must keep in mind how much space is needed now and in the future. Electrical power and air supply, security needs for hardware and software, and temperature need to be analyzed when planning for CD-ROM workstations.

Microcomputer workstations requirements are not the same as those for traditional workstations. The lighting requirements, desk height requirements, temperature, and even the type of chair recommended may vary from the traditional workstations. The computers should be positioned so that the monitors are approximately at eye level. The user should be as comfortable as possible and should have everything available at his workstation to complete his search. Ideally, a library would have several CD-ROM workstations in the reference area of the library with each station specializing in a specific discipline. For example, #1 workstation could have all reference materials such as encyclopedias, almanacs, dictionaries, etc. available. This workstation could allow for "selection menu" control which provides the user with options when accessing information from this workstation. The menu would allow access to dictionary, almanac, encyclopedia, atlas, quotation, and other specialized information without leaving this station. The printer could immediately print the available information for the user.

The #2 workstation could access all periodical indexes and full text. The user could determine the index needed by the discipline or subject being studied. For example, if the user is studying literature, the user could use the *Humanities Index* produced by Wilson. If the user is searching for general information, the *Readers' Guide to Periodical Literature* by Wilson, *Infotrac* by Information Access, or *Primary Search* by EBSCO Publishing could be used at this workstation. The

CD-ROM selection menu could provide these indexes and access full text information from this workstation. The directions and manuals should be available at the station. *If* the user has a problem accessing the information a reference librarian will be available.

Workstation #3 could provide all science databases and full text information focusing on science. CD-ROM sources, such as *Sirs, Facts on File, Newsbank, Applied Science and Technology, Infotrac,* and *EBSCO Publishing* provide excellent scientific, factual information which can inform the user. The menu will allow the user to manipulate the learning environment for instant information.

However, if there is only one available workstation the selection menu can still provide access to several different databases. This station, for example, could provide periodical indexes, newspaper texts, encyclopedia and other reference materials. The librarian would have to organize available scheduling to meet the students' and teachers' educational needs if there is only one station available, but this can be done and it has worked well in some academic environments. As the school or library adds the CD-ROM technology the library can customize the workstations to make the search process successful for the user.

Other considerations when planning for location of the technology are traffic, noise, location of educators and librarians to the station, dust, space for handicapped, and additional space for specific operational manuals.

Manuals and directions for information access should be made available at each station. When writing directions the following suggestions may be considered: (1) Use special dictionaries or subject guides to help the user with special searching vocabulary; (2) Choose the terms the user will need to access the information; (3) Think of key words or alternate words for the subject; (4) Consult the reference librarian for suggestions if the user needs help; (5) Begin with general terms and then go to specifics; (6) The most useful suggestion is to ask the librarian for help.

Following are questions and guidelines that should be studied by persons who are considering purchasing and developing a CD-ROM system. Equipment criteria and evaluation points are given as well as a survey that will help librarians determine their library's specific needs.

Examples for accessing specific databases such as *Infotrac,* H. W. Wilson's Databases and *Primary Search* from EBSCO are also provided for the teacher and librarian. Explanations of these directions may be given to the students before their research. This instruction may eliminate user frustration especially if the user is not familiar with using CD-ROM databases. These instructions may also assist the teacher who might be reluctant to work with this technology.

Collection Development Policy

Requests for CD-ROM products should be reviewed by a committee composed of teachers, librarians, administrators, and parents. These products should be considered on the basis of their merit. The following criteria will be considered in making purchasing decisions: reliability, authenticity, appropriateness, format, accessibility, technical aspects, and physical characteristics.

The first step in database selection is a written policy from a selection committee on the needs, responsibilities, and objectives of the school. With this written policy the selection committee can begin to evaluate CD-ROM products for relevance and accessibility. The following are criteria that can be used to assist the media professional and the teacher in previewing products. Each criteria is followed by a list of questions.

Reliability/Authenticity

1. Is the information factual and does it include documentation?
2. Does the information promote the user's or school's objectives?
3. Does the information promote multicultural views?
4. Does the information promote the minority viewpoint?
5. Is the information dated (automobiles, clothing, etc.)?
6. Does the information avoid stereotyping of religion, sex, race, etc.?

Appropriateness

1. Is the language appropriate for teacher's goals and objectives?
2. Is the vocabulary appropriate for the student's grade level or assignment?
3. Is the information motivational to the student?
4. Does the information provide for collaborative learning as well as for individualization?
5. Does the information provide for student's response?
6. Are skills, concepts, and generalizations appropriate for students?
7. Is content and presentation considered together?

Format

1. Is the information presented in a logical and orderly manner?
2. Is the software easily used?

3. Is the quality (visual and audio) appropriate?
4. Does the menu provide clear explanations?

Accessibility

1. Is the material easy to access?
2. Does the producer provide a user's or teacher's guide?
3. Are the directions clear and logical?

Technical Aspects

1. Is the software easy to install?
2. Are the color and focus clear?
3. Is there extraneous visual information?
4. Is the color necessary to the behavioral objective?

Physical Characteristics

1. Will the material survive heavy use and student handling?
2. Are the products guaranteed?

CD-ROM Equipment Criteria

The selection committee will concentrate on the following criteria for evaluating equipment.

Reliability

1. Past performance record and reliability
2. Adequate customer support service for training and technical support
3. List of customers in the committee's district for references

Compatibility

1. Is the equipment compatible within the school? System?
2. Is the equipment compatible within the network?
3. Is the equipment compatible with the CD-ROM products?
4. Is the equipment compatible with future planning of CD-ROM technology?

Cost

1. One-time cost or annual subscription cost
2. Equipment training cost
3. Equipment maintenance and reference support
4. Future local networking cost

Printer Evaluation

Questions to consider when selecting a printer:
1. Is the printer manufactured by a reliable company?
2. Does the printer support multiple print modes?
3. Is the printer simple to install and operate?
4. Is the printer's documentation comprehensible?
5. Is the annual cost of replacement ribbons, ink cartridges, or toner compatible with other manufacturers' prices?
6. Can the printer be used on a network?
7. Is the quality of the print clear?

The following CD-ROM evaluation can be used to analyze your program and get input from users.

CD-ROM Evaluation

Please circle or fill in the appropriate information.

STATUS: Teacher   Librarian   Student   Other

DATABASE USED: _____

Have you ever used CD-ROM Database before?   YES   NO

Did you ever attend a training session on how to search CD-ROM Databases?   YES   NO

Did library reference staff assist you in learning to use the CD-ROM?   YES   NO

Do you consider your CD-ROM search to have been successful?   YES   NO

Would you use this database again?   YES   NO

How familiar are you with personal computers?

| NOT | SOMEWHAT | VERY |
| FAMILIAR | FAMILIAR | FAMILIAR |

How did you learn about the CD-ROM service?

FLIER   NEWSPAPER   FRIEND   LIBRARIAN
                BULLETIN BOARD

Please circle the word to which you agree or disagree.

The CD-ROM was easy to learn and use.

AGREE   NEUTRAL   DISAGREE

The reference guide card was helpful.

AGREE   NEUTRAL   DISAGREE

The user manual was helpful.

AGREE   NEUTRAL   DISAGREE

Students could use the CD-ROM Index without training.

AGREE   NEUTRAL   DISAGREE

Estimate time used: _____ 0-10 min.   _____20-30 min.
                        _____10-20 min.   _____30+ min.

Library Computer Survey

1. Which computer databases have you used?

   _____*Applied Science & Technology*

   _____*Books in Print*

   _____*Business Periodicals*

   _____*ERIC*

   _____*Essay & General Literature*

   _____*Humanities Index*

_____*InfoTrac*
_____*Intelligent Catalog*
_____*MAS (EBSCO)*
_____*Readers' Guide to Periodicals Abstracts*
_____OTHER

2. Did you find what you needed?   YES   NO

3. Did you get help from a library staff member?
   YES   NO

4. What subjects did you research?
   _____Science
   _____Literature
   _____History
   _____Current Events
   _____Politics
   _____Social Science

Accessing Specific Databases

LESSON PLAN

Goals:
> To introduce students to electronic research.
> To acquaint students with logical operators and to narrow or broaden a search.
> To teach students to assess and use the results of their search.

Objectives:
> Students will learn the techniques and methods of searching CD-ROM information.
> Students will learn to search authors, titles, and subjects.
> Students will use search results.

Activities:
> Teacher will explain the operation of electronic research.
> Teacher will explain the menu and the options available at the work stations.

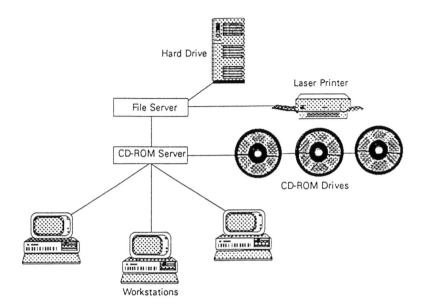

The most difficult part of conducting a successful search is selecting the correct term or terms and knowing how to combine them. This requires the students to think critically about what they want to accomplish from the search. The students may combine terms using what is called Boolean logic which refers back to the set theory. In order to narrow the search the sets can be combined using "and," "or," or "not."

Most CD-ROM databases have some form of controlled vocabulary. However, the student will have to think of key words or alternate words for the topic being searched. For example, the user may be searching *Lasers and Weapons* in periodicals.

STEP 1: LOOK AT THE TOP OF THE COMPUTER SCREEN.

CHECK TO SEE IF THE CORRECT CD-ROM IS IN THE COMPUTER.

STEP 2: TYPE IN YOUR SUBJECT.

Press **Esc** to choose a different database to search.

```
┌──────────────── SEARCH HEADING ──────────────┐
│                                               │
│      Enter the subject or name you wish to find:  │
│                                               │
│       ┌───────────────────────────────┐       │
│       │                               │       │
│       │                               │       │
│       │                               │       │
│       └───────────────────────────────┘       │
│                                               │
│            then press **Enter** to search.        │
│                                               │
└───────────────────────────────────────────────┘
```

```
┌───────────────────────────────────────────┐
│                                           │
│            LASERS  AND  WEAPONS           │
│                                           │
└───────────────────────────────────────────┘
```

then press **Enter** to search.

STEP 3:   PRESS ENTER TO SEE ENTRIES FOR
          HIGHLIGHTING SUBJECTS

Entries	*Subject*
20	Lasers
10	Laser/History
2	Lasers/Patents
10	Lasers/Weapons

STEP 4:   PUT THE CURSER ON THE LINE YOU
          WISH TO SEARCH:

```
┌───────────────────────────────────────────┐
│                                           │
│            LASERS/WEAPONS                 │
│                                           │
└───────────────────────────────────────────┘
```

then press **Enter** to search.

STEP 5: PRESS THE ENTER KEY
Laser and weapons, by Douglas Mcgrath il
v252 The Nation Jan 7 '92 p16(3)

PRESS ENTER   LIBRARY SUBSCRIBES

STEP 6: CHECK TO SEE IF YOUR LIBRARY HAS
THE INFORMATION NEEDED OR IF
FULL TEXT, DECIDE IF YOU WANT
THIS INFORMATION

PRESS **Enter**

STEP 7: IF YES, PRINT THE CITATION (OR
FULL TEXT)

STEP 8: IF NO, PRESS **Esc** TO RESUME
BROWSING.

Search Strategies/Tips

To search by subject, type in the complete name. If a person's name is the subject, type the last name first. Example: Jordan, Michael
Not only can you search by SUBJECT, you can also search for people, places, events, or things.

TO SEARCH FOR PEOPLE – SEARCH BY LAST NAME FOR AUTHORS, POLITICIANS OR POLITICAL GROUPS, MOVIE STARS, PEOPLE IN THE NEWS, SPORTS FIGURES AND COMPANIES. Examples: Cosby, Bill; Thatcher, Margaret; National Broadcast Communications, Inc.; Cleveland Indians; Khmer Rouge

TO SEARCH FOR PLACES – SEARCH BY THE CURRENT/ OFFICIAL NAME FOR COUNTRIES, CITIES, STATES, PROV- INCES, ETC. Examples: France; Texas; Chattanooga, Tennessee

TO SEARCH FOR EVENTS – SEARCH BY THE MOST POPU- LAR NAME THE NEWS MEDIA USES FOR AN EVENT. Ex- amples: STAR WARS, *Challenger* (Space Shuttle), Vietnam War

TO SEARCH FOR THINGS – SEARCH BY NAME FOR CON-
SUMER PRODUCTS, COMPUTER PROGRAMS, ETC.   Examples: Coca-Cola (soft drink), Clue (video game)

TO SEARCH FOR ENTERTAINMENT – SEARCH BY SPECIFIC
NAME OF BOOKS, PLAYS, RESTAURANTS.   Examples:
McDonald's (food), Olive Garden (food), *Glamour* (magazine), *The
Atlanta Journal and Constitution* (newspaper), *The King and I* (play)

TO SEARCH BY AUTHOR, TYPE IN THE LAST NAME
FIRST. Examples: Walker, Alice (author), Twain, Mark (author),
Clancy, Tom (author)

The user will access information from CD-ROM resources by using
key terms. The producers decide upon the terms which will access the information. Therefore, the user cannot access all information by using
the same terms for all databases or CD-ROM programs. For example, the
ERIC database has the following sub-terms under ETHNIC GROUPS
AND DISADVANTAGED. Compare the same sub-terms with *Infotrac* database. The following list of descriptors or subjects may be
compared because they are used by two different producers.

ERIC Index
Ethnic Groups and Disadvantaged:
Descriptors to Use

Acculturation	Hispanic Americans
American Indians	Indians
Arabs	Italian Americans
Chinese Americans	Jews
Cultural Awareness	Mexican Americans
Cultural Differences	Migrant Children
Disadvantaged	Migrant Education
Disadvantaged Youth	Migrants
Ethnic Groups	Social Integration
Ethnicity	Socioeconomic Background

Infotrac
Ethnic Groups and Disadvantaged:
Subjects to Use

Amerasians
Arab Americans
Asians
Cherokee Indians (also other
   specific tribes of Indians)
Children of Migrant Laborers
Chinese
Chinese American Children
Chinese Americans
Education, Bilingual
Ethnic Groups — Educations

Hispanic American Children
Indians
Indians of North America —
   Education
Jews
Italian Americans
Mexican American Youth
Mexican Americans
Minorities — Education
Refugees
Socially Handicapped Children

Practice

1. Place check marks beside the two subjects which mean nearly the same thing.

_____(a)   cats
_____(b)   popcorn
_____(c)   preschool
_____(d)   kindergarten

2. Place a check mark beside the one word which is a more specific term than cat.

_____(a)   animal
_____(b)   whale
_____(c)   Siamese cat
_____(d)   lion

3. Place a check mark beside the one subject which is a term more general than hamburger.

_____(a)   meat
_____(b)   cheeseburger
_____(c)   ground beef
_____(d)   burger

4. Place a check mark beside the one subject which is a term more general than "crack."

_____(a)   drug
_____(b)   alcohol
_____(c)   marijuana
_____(d)   cigarette

5. Place a check mark beside the one subject which is more specific than mammal.

_____(a)   insect
_____(b)   species
_____(c)   amphibian
_____(d)   cow

6. Place check marks beside the two subjects which mean nearly the same thing.

_____(a)   book
_____(b)   pamphlet
_____(c)   record
_____(d)   audio

Menu Commands

It is very important to read the directions and menu commands for each specific CD-ROM database. However, the function keys are the same on several database menus. Preview these function keys before a search is conducted. The practice of reviewing these special features may provide for a more successful search.

Examples of Menu Commands

Return Key   To enter your search terms, or display or
ESC   To see a LIST OF COMMANDS.

To BROADEN your search:

A. Use truncation (*)   FIND: homeless*
                               also retrieves homelessness

B. Link terms using OR   FIND: homeless* or jobless*

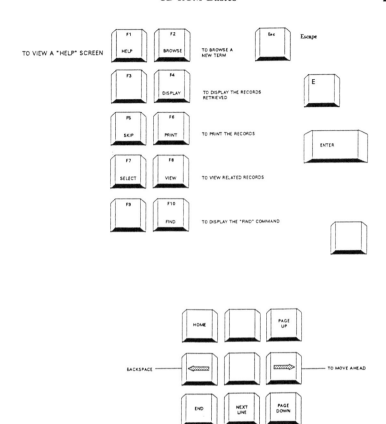

Menu commands

Or — retrieves records in which either or both of the terms appear.

To NARROW your search:

A. Combine terms using:

And — both terms in same record   FIND: homeless and unemployment

With — both terms in same field   FIND: homeless with shelters

Near — both terms in same sentence   FIND: homeless near families

Not — first term but not second   FIND: homeless not mental
    term   illness

B. Use field codes

TI — title   FIND: homeless in ti
DE — descriptor listed in data-   FIND: mental-illness in de
    base thesaurus: use hyphen
    to join multi-word descrip-
    tors
PY — limits by year of publica-   FIND: homeless in py   1988
    tion or a range of years   FIND: homeless in py = 1985–
                                                          1988
                                                      FIND: homeless in py = 1986

C. Combine several concepts

( ) — use parentheses to group   FIND: (homeless not mental ill-
    your concepts   ness in de) and

Basic Commands

F1   to "help"
F2   to "find"
F3   to change discs or "guide"
F4   to "show"
F5   to view index or alphabetical lists
F7   to "restart"
F8   to view related terms
F10   to display last command

TWO
Distributors

Before selecting a distributor it is important to check in your area and try to find one which has demonstrated reliability and dependability. If the distributor cannot provide a list of satisfied customers, please conduct further research until a vendor is located which has a record of good performance. Mail order distributors are probably the least desirable choice for purchasing computer equipment because of limited service. However, if the company has a good record and provides high quality telephone support service, this may be a bonus. Below is a list of questions to consider when selecting a distributor for CD-ROM products and equipment.

1. Does the distributor provide lease/purchase options?
2. Does the distributor provide maintenance for equipment?
3. Does the distributor provide a toll-free telephone number?
4. Does the distributor provide free training sessions?
5. Does the distributor provide maintenance agreements?
6. Does the distributor provide copyright and multi-restrictions?
7. Does the distributor have other relevant databases?
8. Does the distributor demonstrate good performance?
9. Does the distributor communicate well with the customer?

CD-ROM Distributors and Producers

Distributors

Abt Books, Inc.
146 Mt. Auburn St.
Cambridge, MA 02138
(617) 661-1300
Sells and rents some 60 CD-ROM databases including European.

23

Bureau of Electronic Publishing
141 New Road
Parsippany, NJ 07054
1-800-828-4766

CDiscovery
Computerworks of Northport
260 Main St.
Northport, NY 11768
1-800-825-DISK

CD One Stop
13 F. J. Clarke Circle
Bethel, CT 06801
1-800-826-0079
Wholesaler — compact discs.

CD-ROM INC.
1667 Cole Boulevard, Suite 400
Golden, CO 80401
(303) 231-9373

Compact Disk Products, Inc.
223 E. 85th St.
New York, NY 10028
(212) 737-8400; FAX (212) 737-8289

EBSCO Publishing
P.O. Box 1943
Birmingham, AL 35201
1-800-826-3024, (205) 991-1182; FAX (508) 887-3923
A producer and distributor of CD-ROM products.

FAXON Co.
15 Southwest Park
Westbrook, MA 02090
1-800-44-FAXON, (617) 329-3350; FAX (617) 326-5484
FAXON issues Access Faxon.

Gale Research, Inc.
P.O. Box 33477
Detroit, MI 48232-5477
1-800-877-GALE

New Media Source
Suite 2153
3830 Valley Centre Drive
San Diego, CA 92130-9834
1-800-344-2621

UPDATA
1736 Westwood Blvd.
Los Angeles, CA 90024
1-800-882-2844

University of Colorado
LASP-Campus Box 392
Boulder, CO 80309
(303) 492-7666

Ztek Co.
P.O. Box 1968
Lexington, KY 40593
1-800-247-1603, (606) 252-7276
CD-ROM products and videodiscs produced primarily for the education
market.

Producers

Abt Books, Inc.
146 Mt. Auburn St.
Cambridge, MA 02138
(617) 661-1300
Products: Real estate transfer database; National Portrait Gallery, The
Permanent Collection

Access Innovations, Inc.
P.O. Box 40130
4320 Mesa Grande S.E.
Albuquerque, NM 87196
1-800-421-8711, (505) 265-3591
Product: A-V ONLINE

Activism
2350 Bayshore Pkwy.
Mountain View, CA 94043
1-800-227-6900, (415) 960-0410
Product: Manhole (Mac)

AIRS, Inc.
Engineering Research Center
335 Paint Branch Drive
College Park, MD 20741
(301) 454-2022
Product: Bible Library

Alde Publishing
4830 W. 77th St.
P.O. Box 35326
Minneapolis, MN 55435
(612) 835-5240; FAX (612) 835-3401

American Library Association
Information Technology Publishing
50 E. Huron St.
Chicago, IL 60611
1-800-545-2433, (312) 955-6780
Product: ALA CD-ROM

American Mathematical Society
P.O. Box 6248
Providence, RI 02940
1-800-556-7774, (401) 272-9500
Product: MathSciDisc

American Psychological Association
750 1st St. NE
Washington, DC 20002-4242
1-800-374-2721
Product: PsycLit

AMIGOS Bibliographic Council, Inc.
11300 N. Central Expressway, Suite 321
Dallas, TX 75243
1-800-843-8482, (214) 759-6130
Product: OCLC/AMIGOS Collection Analysis CD

Amtec Information Services
3700 Industry Ave.
Lakewood, CA 90714-6050
(213) 595-4756
Products: Exxon Corp. Basic Practices Manual; GE Aircraft Engines;
    Mack Electronic Parts Disc

Apple Computer
20525 Mariani Ave.
Cupertino, CA 95014
(408) 973-6025
Product: Apple Science CD Volume 1

Aries Systems Corp.
79 Boxford St.
North Andover, MA 01845-3219
(508) 689-9334
Products: CancerLit; Medline-Knowledge Finder (IBM & Mac)

Auto-Graphics, Inc.
3201 Temple Ave.
Pomona, CA 91768
1-800-325-7961, (714) 595-7207
Products: GDCS Impact; Impact

Baker & Taylor
50 Kirby Ave.
Somerville, NJ 08876
1-800-526-3811; 1-800-352-4841 (in N.J.); 1-800-524-2486 (in Canada)
Product: BaTaSYSTEMS Order

Bell & Howell
5700 Lombardo Center
Suite 220
Seven Hills, OH 44131
(216) 642-9060
Products: Chrysler Parts Catalog; GM Parts Catalog; Honda Parts
    Catalog; Mercedes-Benz

Berkeley Macintosh User Group (BMUG)
2150 Kettredge 3b
Berkeley, CA 94709
(415) 549-2684
Product: CD-ROM (MAC)

BIOSIS
2100 Arch St.
Philadelphia, PA 19103-1399
1-800-523-4806, (215) 587-4800; FAX (215) 587-2016
Product: Biological Abstracts

Blackwell North America, Inc.
6024 SW Jean Rd.

Bldg. G.
Lake Oswego, OR 97035
(503) 684-1140
Product: PC Order Plus

Bowker Electronic Publishing
245 W. 17th St.
New York, NY 10011
1-800-323-3288; (212) 337-6989; FAX (212) 645-0475
Products: Books in Print Plus (IBM/Mac); Books in print with book
review plus; Books out of print plus; Ulrich's plus; Variety's Video
Directory Plus

Brodart Automation
500 Arch St.
Williamsport, PA 17705
1-800-233-8467, (717) 326-2461
Products: ACCESS Pennsylvania; LePac; Government Documents Op-
tion; LePac: Interlibrary Loan; PC Rose System

Broderbund Software
17 Paul Dr.
San Rafael, CA 94903
(415) 479-1170
Product: Whole Earth Learning Disc (IBM/Mac)

Buchändler Vereinigung-GMBH
Gro Ber Hirschraben 17-21
Postfach 100442
6000 Frankfurt am Main 1, West Germany
Product: Verzeichnis Lieferbarer Bucher (German Books in Print sold
by Chadwyck-Healy)

Buckmaster Publishing
Route 3
Box 56
Mineral, VA 23117
1-800-282-5628, (703) 894-5777
Product: Place-Name Index

C.A.B. International
Farnham House
Farnham Royal
Slough S12 3BN England
Product: CAB Abstracts

CD/Law Reports, Inc.
305 S. Hale, Suite 1
Wheaton, IL 60187
(312) 668-8895
Products: CD/LAW: Illinois; Laserlaw Series

CD Plus
2901 Broadway, Suite 154
New York, NY 10025
(212) 932-1485
Products: CancerLit; Health; Medline—CD Plus

CMC ReSearch
7150 S.W. Hampton, Suite 120
Portland, OR 97223
(503) 639-3395
Products: Cancer on Disc: 1988; Journal of Radiology; Pediatrics on Disc; Sherlock Holmes on Disc; Yearbook

Compact Cambridge
Cambridge Information Group
7200 Wisconsin Ave.
Bethesda, MD 20814
1-800-227-3052, (301) 961-6700
Products: Aquatic Sciences and Fisheries; CancerLit CD-ROM; Drug Information Center; Life Sciences Collection; Medline—Compact Cambridge; PDQ CD-ROM (Physicians' Data Query)

Compact Discoveries, Inc.
1050 S. Federal Highway
Delray Beach, FL 33444
(305) 243-1453
Products: Images Demo; Yellow Page Demo

Computer Access Corp.
26 Brighton St., Suite 324
Belmont, MA 02178
(617) 484-2412
Product: CD-ROM: The New Papyrus

Computer Aided Planning, Inc.
169-C Monroe N.W.
Grand Rapids, MI 49503
(616) 454-0000
Product: CAP (Computer Aided Programming)

Comstock, Inc.
30 Irving Pl.
New York, NY 10003
(212) 353-8686
Product: Desktop Photography (Mac)

Congressional Information Service, Inc.
4520 East-West Highway, Suite 800
Bethesda, MD 20814-1550
1-800-638-8380, (301) 654-1550
Product: CIS Congressional Masterfile 1789-1969

Cornell University Distribution Center
7 Research Park
Ithaca, NY 14850
(607) 255-2901
Product: Black Fiction Up to 1920

Data Base Products, Inc.
12770 Coit Road, Suite 1111
Dallas, TX 75251-1314
1-800-345-2876, (214) 233-0595
Products: Form 41: Airline Carrier Filings; International: Airline
    Traffic; Itineraries; O & D Plus Historical; Onboard: Airline Traffic
    Data

DataTimes
1400 Quail Springs Pkwy., #450
Oklahoma City, OK 73134
(405) 451-6400
Products: *Daily Oklahoman*; Data Times Libraries System; *Washington
    Post*

Delorme Mapping Systems
P.O. Box 298
Freeport, ME 04032
(207) 865-4171
Product: Delorme's World Atlas

Deutsche Bibelgesellschaft
Balingerstrasse 31
7000 Stuttgart 80 East Germany
(49) 0711 71810
Product: Luther Bible

DIALOG Information Services
3460 Hillview Ave.
Palo Alto, CA 94304
1-800-3-DIALOG, (415) 858-3985
Products: DIALOG Ondisc; Canadian Business and Current Affairs; ERIC; Medline: Medline Clinical Collection: NTIS; Standard and Poor's Corporations.

Digital Diagnostics, Inc.
601 University Ave.
Sacramento, CA 95825
1-800-826-5595, (916) 921-6629
Products: AIDS Supplement; Medline-BiblioMed; Medline-BiblioMed with AIDS Supplement; MetroScan

Digital Directory Assistance
5161 River Rd.
Bethesda, MD 20816
(301) 657-8548
Product: Phone Disc

Disclosure
5161 River Rd.
Bethesda, MD 20816
1-800-843-7747, (301) 951-1300
Products: Compact Disclosure; Compact Disclosure—Europe; Disclosure Spectrum; Laser Disclosure: Commercial, Not for Profit, Wall Street

Discovery Systems
47001 Discovery Blvd.
Dublin, OH 43017
(614) 761-2000
Products: CD-ROM Sampler; Macintosh Showcase

Diversified Data Resources, Inc.
6609 Rosecraft P.I.
Falls Church, VA 22043-1828
(202) 237-0682
Products: The Sourcedisc

Donnelley Marketing Information Services
70 Seaview Ave.
P.O. Box 10250
Stamford, CT 06904

1-800-527-3647, (203) 353-7474
Product: Conquest: Consumer Information

Dun's Marketing Service
49 Old Bloomfield Rd.
Mountain Lakes, NJ 07046
1-800-526-0651, (201) 299-0181
Products: Cataloger's Tool Kit; Comprehensive Medline; Core Medline; Reference Tool Kit; The Serials Directory

EBSCO Electronic Information
P.O. Box 325
Topsfield, MA 01983
1-800-221-1826, (508) 887-6667
Products: Cataloger's Tool Kit; Comprehensive Medline; Core Medline; Reference Tool Kit; The Serials Directory

Education Systems Corp.
6170 Cornerstone Court East, Suite 300
San Diego, CA 92121-3170
(619) 587-0087
Product: ESC Integrated Learning System

Educorp USA
531 Stephens Ave., Suite B
Solana Beach, CA 92075
1-800-843-9497, (619) 259-0255
Product: Public Domain Mac Programs (Macintosh)

Electromap, Inc.
P.O. Box 1153
Fayetteville, AR 72702-1153
Product: World Atlas

Electronic Text Corporation
2500 N. University Ave.
Provo, UT 84604
(801) 226-0616
Product: American Authors on CD-ROM

H. W. Wilson Co.
950 University Ave.
Bronx, NY 10452
(212) 588-8400
Products: Applied Science & Technology Index; Art Index; Biography

Index; Biological and Agricultural Index; Book Review Digest; Business Periodicals Index; Cumulative Book Index; Education Index; Essay and General Literature Index; Film Literature Index; General Science Index; GPO Monthly Catalog Index to Government Periodicals; Humanities Index; Index to Legal Periodicals; Library Literature; Modern Language Association Index; Readers' Guide Abstracts; Reader's Guide to Periodical Literature; Social Science Index; WILSONDISC Demonstration Disc

Virginia Polytechnic Institute
Blacksburg, VA 24061
(703) 231-6000
Product: Virginia Disk

Voyager Co.
1351 Pacific Coast Hwy.
Santa Monica, CA 90401
(213) 451-1383
Product: CD Companion — Beethoven Symphony No. 9

Walters Lexicon Co.
Sodermalmstrong 8,
17800 Stockholm, Sweden
Product: Termdok

WeatherDisk Associates, Inc.
4584 N.E. 89th St.
Seattle, WA 98115
(206) 524-4314
Product: World WeatherDisk

West Publishing Co.
P.O. Box 64526
St. Paul, MN 55164-0526
(612) 228-2497
Products: West CD-ROM Bankruptcy Library; West CD-ROM Federal
   Civil Practice Library; West CD-ROM Government Contracts Library;
   West CD-ROM Libraries

Western Library Network
Washington State Library
Mail Stop AJ-11W
Olympia, WA 98504-0111
(206) 459-6518; FAX (206) 459-6341
Product: LaserCat

J. Whitaker & Sons Ltd.
BookBank on CD-ROM
12 Dyott St.
London WCIA 1Df, England
(44) 1-836-8911
Product: BookBank

Wiley Electronic Publishing
605 Third Ave.
New York, NY 10158-0012
(212) 850-6509
Products: Encyclopedia of Polymer Science and Engineering; International Dictionary of Medicine and Biology; Kirk-Othmer Encyclopedia of Chemical Technology; Registry of Mass Spectral Data

Wright Investors' Service (WIS)
10 Middle St.
Bridgeport, CT 06604
(203) 333-6666
Product: Worldscope Profiles

Xiphias
Helms Hall
875 Venice Blvd.
Los Angeles, CA 90034
(213) 821-0074
Products: National Telephone Directory (Mac); Time Table of History/ Science & Innovation (Mac)

Ziff Communications
1 Par Ave.
New York, NY 10016
(212) 503-4400
Product: Computer Library

Ziff Davis Technical Information Co.
80 Blanchard Rd.
Burlington, MA 01830
(617) 273-5500
Product: Haystack: Logistics, Procurement, Engineering Files

Manufacturers of CD-ROM Drives

Amdek Corp.
1901 Zanker Rd.
San Jose, CA 95112
(408) 636-8570
Model: Laserdek 1000*; Laserdek 2000*

Apple Computer
20525 Mariani Ave.
Cupertino, CA 95014
(408) 745-2000
Model: AppleCD SC (Sony drive, $1,199)

Chinon America, Inc.
660 Maple Ave.
Torrance, CA 90503
(213) 533-0274
Model: CDS-430*

Denon
222 New Rd.
Parsippany, NJ 07054
(201) 575-7810
Model: DRD-250 (Sony Drive*); DRD-251 (Sony Drive*); DRD-253 (Sony Drive*); DRD-550 (Denon Drive*)

Digital Equipment Corp.
10 Tara Blvd.
Nashua, NH 03062
(603) 884-2166
Model: RRD50-AA ($1,000); RRD50-EA ($1,200); RRD50-QA ($1,200)

Hitachi
401 W. Artesia Blvd.
Compton, CA 90220
1-800-262-1502, (213) 537-8383
Model: CDR-1502S ($899); CDR-1503S ($899); CDR-1553S ($1,199); CDR-2500 ($899); CDR-3500 (Sony $875)

JVC
41 Slater Dr.
Elmwood Park, NJ 07407
(201) 794-3900
Model: XR-R100*; XR-R1001*

Laser Magnetic Storage International (MSI)
4425 Arrows West Dr.
Colorado Springs, CO 80907
(303) 593-4269, (303) 593-4270
Model: CM121 (Philips, $820); CM131 (Philips, $1,130); CM132 (Philips, $1,190); CM201 (Philips*); CM210 (Philips*)

NEC Home Electronics
1255 Michael Dr.
Wood Dale, IL 60191
(312) 860-9500
Model: Intersect CDR-77 ($999); Intersect CDR-80 ($899)

Panasonic
1 Panasonic Way
Secaucus, NJ 07094
(201) 392-4602
Model: SQ-D1 ($999); SQ-D101 ($1,149)

Philips Information Systems, Inc.
2111 Wilson Blvd., Suite 435
Arlington, VA 22201
(703) 875-2222
Model: CM100; CM110; CM121; CM201; CM210

Reference Technology
5700 Flatiron Pkwy.
Boulder, CO 80301
(303) 449-4157
Model: Clasix 500 ($990)

* Original Equipment Manufacturer

Librarians' Advice to Educators When Selecting CD-ROM Databases

1. The buyer needs to call the 1-800 numbers and get free catalogs from distributors.
2. Get several catalogs in your subject area.
3. Prices will vary and CD-ROM software packages will vary from distributors.
4. Call the 1-800 numbers of publishers and get feedback addressing

your specific educational objectives. If you are not satisfied with the conversation do not use that distributor or product. *Shop around.*

5. Support services are crucial when purchasing CD-ROM equipment and products.

6. The buyer needs to check with the distributor regarding software and hardware requirements to insure that the program will run on available equipment.

7. This handbook includes operating specifications for each program. When Mac is indicated, it may be possible to run these programs on Apple. Again, consult with the distributor to determine compatibility.

8. Do not feel foolish or inadequate when researching CD-ROM products for purchase. The technology changes rapidly and it is impossible to know everything. Write your goals and objectives and then find a distributor who will work with you and answer your questions. The end result, students' success, is worth the effort.

9. Begin with the simple system, one which you can network or add to, and work into a more sophisticated electronic informational center.

10. Keep in mind the age groups and academic levels of the students when selecting materials.

THREE
Databases

We would like to express our appreciation to the distributors who have contributed reviews and information: EBSCO, Ztek, CDiscovery, Updata, CD-ROM, Inc., H. W. Wilson, Sirs, Information Access and Bureau of Electronic Publishing. As academic librarians we have concentrated on educational materials to meet the objectives of classroom teachers from kindergarten through college. The following programs are appropriate for the educational community and have been researched, reviewed, previewed, and utilized by students. Good luck!

AEROSPACE

Accident/Incident Archive. Operating System: PC; *Subject:* Aerospace; *Price:* $995; *Grade Level:* General; *Hardware:* See distributor; *Software:* See distributor; *Distributor:* CD-ROM, Inc.

This is a complete reference to every aircraft accident or incident since 1970. Details on the aircraft, pilot, weather, location, cause, contributing factors, and more. This disc is fully indexed for customized searches and is updated annually.

Aerospace. Producer: DIALOG Information Services; *Operating System:* PC; *Subject:* Aerospace; *Price:* Annual subscription – $3450; annual subscription – Print Subscribers – $2760; annual subscription for LAN – $6900; annual subscription/print subs. for LAN $5520; *Grade Level:* General; *Hardware:* IBM PC compatible; 640 K RAM; 10 MB hard disk recommended; CD-ROM player; printer for text (optional) CD player; *Software:* PC-DOS or MS-DOS, Microsoft CD-ROM extensions; *Distributor:* EBSCO.

International coverage of scientific and technical literature related to aerospace engineering. Includes: atmospheric and space sciences; aerodynamics; aircraft and aerospace systems; communications and navigation; propulsion; energy production and conversion; structural engineering and analysis; and laser and robotic technology.

The Aircraft Encyclopedia. Producer: Quanta Press; *Operating System:* PC; *Subject:* Aerospace; *Price:* $136.50; *Grade Level:* JH, HS, C; *Hardware:* IBM PC or compatible; CD-ROM player, card, cable; VGA monitor and card for color; images (optional); monochrome monitor; *Software:* PC-DOS or MS-DOS 2.1 or higher, Microsoft CD-ROM extensions; *Distributor:* EBSCO

A visual compendia of worldwide military aircraft. Contains a detailed database of NATO, Warsaw Pact, and other nations, military aircraft. The database is complemented by line drawings, black and white photographs, and VGA color images. Includes information on country of origin, model, name, manufacturer, crew, mission, wing-span, length, speed, range, and ceiling.

Space Series: Apollo. Producer: NASA; *Operating system:* PC/MAC; *Subject:* Apollo Space Program; *Price:* $124; *Grade Level:* General; *Hardware:* IBM PC/MAC Plus; *Software:* See distributor; *Distributor:* UPDATA.

This historical database covers the Apollo space program from the early rocket pioneering of the 1920s until the joint Apollo-Soyuz space venture. Information was gathered from NASA publications, briefings, and ex-employee interviews. Major areas covered include chronology, equipment, foreign programs, probes and satellites, and astronauts and cosmonauts. Hundreds of photographs are included as well as a glossary. This disc contains a wealth of information on how mankind got to the moon. For use by both professionals and students.

AGRICULTURE

Agri/Stats I. Producer: Hopkins Technology; *Operating System:* PC; *Subject:* Agriculture; *Price:* $65; *Grade Level:* General; *Hardware:* IBM PC or compatible; 512K RAM; CD-ROM; *Software:* PC-DOS or MS-DOS version 3.1, 3.3 or higher, Microsoft CD-ROM extensions; *Distributor:* EBSCO.

Eight agricultural databases of U.S. statistics including crop estimates, grain stocks, country estimates — crops and livestock, hog and pig estimates, cattle inventory and cattle on feed. Bonus: corn production in 42 African countries since 1966. There are over 700,000 individual records in these databases comprising millions of individual data points, some as far back as 1939.

Agricultural Statistics. Producer: Slater Hall Information Products; *Operating System:* PC; *Subject:* Agriculture; *Price:* $745; *Grade Level:*

General; *Hardware:* IBM PC or compatible; 512K RAM; CD-ROM player; *Software:* PC-DOS or MS-DOS 2.1 or higher; *Distributor:* EBSCO. Complete county data from the 1987 Census of Agriculture. Covers farms, acreage, crops, livestock, production, sales, operating expenses, and all other data items contained in the Census Bureau's complete county file. Historical comparisons of 1987 and 1982 census on most items. Farm income from the Commerce Department's regional economic information system, annual data beginning with 1969 and covering income in major receipt and expenditure categories for counties and regions.

AIDS

Aidsline. *Producer:* SilverPlatter Information; *Operating System:* PC; *Subject:* Medicine—AIDS; *Price:* $495; *Grade Level:* JH, HS, C; *Hardware:* IBM PC or compatible; 640K RAM, standard CD-ROM player; monitor; printer (optional); 1 floppy drive; hard disk recommended; *Software:* PC-DOS or MS-DOS 2.1 or higher, Microsoft CD-ROM extensions; *Distributor:* EBSCO.

Consists of information from the U.S. National Library of Medicine's Medline, Health Planning and Administration, and Cancerlit databases. Over 30,000 records are contained from 1980 to the present with over 3,000 journals scanned for inclusion. Detailed coverage of all aspects of the AIDS crisis is available, focusing on clinical aspects but including health planning implications and cancer research. Journal articles, government/technical reports, meeting abstracts/papers and more are included.

Compact Library: AIDS. *Producer:* Maxwell Electronic Publishing; *Operating System:* PC; *Subject:* Medicine; *Price:* $875; *Grade Level:* JH, HS, C; *Hardware:* IBM XT AT, PS/2 or compatible; 640K RAM; hard disk; CD-ROM player; *Software:* PC-DOS or MS-DOS 3.1 or higher, Microsoft CD-ROM extensions; *Distributor:* EBSCO.

The disc offers an innovative, time-saving approach to searching the medical literature on AIDS. The disc holds a complete library of medical information on AIDS including a growing list of respected resources. The database is continually updated and includes the AIDS Knowledge Base, full text of articles from leading biomedical journals, abstracts from the Bureau of Hygiene and Tropical Diseases AIDS database plus a subset of Medline.

ART

Aquatic Art. *Operating System:* MAC; *Subject:* Art/Sea Life; *Price:* $149; *Grade Level:* JH, HS; *Hardware:* See distributor; *Software:* See distributor; *Distributor:* UPDATA.
Images of marine life from Hawaii and the Caribbean. Dolphins, sea turtles, and tropical fish are presented along with their scientific (Latin) names and a variety of interesting facts. See the bluestriped Butterfly fish and the white spotted Puffer. Images can be viewed in color, copied and exported using Hypercard Interface. Allows for search of keywords. Can be used as an educational toolbelt as well as for publications and presentations.

Art Index. *Producer:* The H. W. Wilson Company; *Operating System:* PC; *Subject:* Art; *Price:* $1495; *Grade Level:* General; *Hardware:* IBM PS/2 series of computers or any IBM PC with 640K RAM; fixed-disk drive or any WILSONLINE Workstation; *Software:* PC-DOS or MS-DOS Microsoft CD-ROM extensions; *Distributor:* EBSCO.
A single-alphabet, subject-author index of 227 domestic and foreign periodicals, yearbooks, and museum bulletins. Extensive cross-referencing. Indexing reflects current terminology. Complete bibliographic data on each article indexed, with notation of illustrations, portraits, diagrams, plans, and charts. Indexes of book reviews.

Clip Art 3-D. *Producer:* NEC; *Operating System:*PC/MAC; *Subject:* Clip Art; *Price:* $399; *Grade Level:* JH, HS; *Hardware:* See distributor; *Software:* See distributor; *Distributor:* Ztek.
Contains over 2500 clip-art images in 3-D covering a variety of categories including geography, transportation, buildings, food, bloody razors, equipment, and human figures. Also included are three-dimensional typefaces and over 500 pre-made composite images. The user can be creative in editing images by changing such factors as position, location, size, lighting, color, and perspective. Customized composites can be built as well. Images can be exported in .PIC, .WMF, or EPS formats for use with desktop publishing programs.

Artroom 4.0. *Producer:* PC; *Subject:* Art; *Price:* $808; *Grade Level:* General; *Hardware:* IBM PC or compatible; 640K RAM; CD player; *Software:* PC-DOS or MS-DOS, Microsoft CD-ROM; *Distributor:* EBSCO.
Contains over 120 MB or Image Club EPS clip-art (over 3,000 images). Each update contains approximately 20-30 MB of new clip-art.

Coate's Art Review—Impressionism. *Producer:* Quanta Press; *Operating System:* PC/MAC; *Subject:* Art; *Price:* $139; *Grade Level:* JH, HS, C; *Hardware:* See distributor; *Software:* See distributor; *Distributor:* EBSCO.

Represents a comprehensive review of impressionist artwork and artists. All of the great masters of impressionism are included on this disc, from Renoir to Gauguin, Degas to Monet, Cassat to Manet. Users can search a comprehensive/artist specific database for artwork, museums/collections, schools, and other relevant information. Images can be viewed within the database. Quanta released the entire 12-volume set of Coate's Art Reviews in 1991.

Comstock Desktop Photography—Vol. I. *Producer:* Comstock Desktop Publishing; *Operating System:* PC; *Subject:* Photography; *Price:* $201; *Grade Level:* JH, HS, C; *Hardware:* IBM PC or compatible; 640K RAM; CD-ROM drive or Macintosh Plus, SE or II SCSI and CD-ROM drive; *Software:* PC-DOS or MS-DOS, Microsoft CD-ROM extensions; *Distributor:* EBSCO.

Volume I contains general subject matter with 449 black and white 256 shades of gray, TIFF files.

Comstock Desktop Photography—Volume II. *Price:* $91. All other information is the same as Volume I.

Volume II includes 100 black and white images taken from Vol. I; however, all subject matter relates to business. All photos are ready for use in desktop publishing or other applications.

Comstock Desktop Photography—Volume III. *Producer:* Comstock Desktop Publishing; *Operating System:* MAC; *Subject:* Photography/ ART; *Price:* $201; *Grade Level:* General; *Hardware:* MAC Plus or higher; *Software:* MAC Extensions; *Distributor:* EBSCO.

Volume III contains 441 color and 441 black and white TIFF files of general interest subjects different from Volume I.

Corel ArtShow '91. *Operating System:* PC; *Subject:* Art; *Price:* $74.95; *Grade Level:* General; *Hardware:* MPC Multimedia PCs; *Software:* CorelDraw 2.0; *Distributor:* New Media Source.

Award Winner CorelDraw features an exciting selection of high quality designs from the second annual Corel/Draw International Design Contest. Over 1,000 stunning images.

EBook's Electronic Library of Art. *Operating System:* MPC; *Subject:* Art; *Price:* $74.95; *Grade Level:* General; *Hardware:* See distributor; *Software:* See distributor; *Distributor:* New Media Source.

Multi-volume series features illustrated multimedia art and humanities CD-ROM, including a wide variety of art images combined into one valuable resource. Subjects covered are painting, sculpture, architecture, photography, design, and theatre.

Events of the 70's and 80's. *Operating System:* MAC; *Subjects:* Arts, Government, Sports; *Price:* $295; *Grade Level:* General; *Hardware:* See distributor; *Software:* See distributor; *Distributor:* CD-ROM, INC.

More than 1500 full-color photographs and three hours of audio of significant world events and important personalities of the period 1970 through 1989.

Experience Bali. *Operating System:* MAC. Subjects: Bali, Religion, Art; *Price:* $39.95; *Grade Level:* General; *Hardware:* See distributor; *Software:* See distributor; *Distributor:* New Media Source.

Beautiful color photographs, animation, and simulation with ambient stereo sound combine to make Experience Bali a memorable interactive experience; view temples, dreams, streets, and vistas; take a music lesson or attend a visually and musically stunning Hindu ceremony.

GEM. *Producer:* Bureau of Electronic Publishing; *Operating System:* MAC; *Subject:* Graphics, Business; *Price:* $99; *Grade Level:* HS; *Hardware:* Macintosh Plus/SE/II portable 1MB RAM System 6.0.2 or higher; *Software:* Partition Driver software from Tranton Systems or Optical Media International is required; *Distributor:* UPDATA.

The GEM (Generous Efforts of Many) provides 620 mb of programs in over 17,000 files which feature art and graphics, sound, business tools, utilities, etc.

National Portrait Gallery. *Operating System:* PC; *Subject:* Art; *Price:* $495; *Grade Level:* JH, HS; *Hardware:* See distributor; *Software:* See distributor; *Distributor:* Bureau of Electronic Publishing.

Contains 3,093 full-color and black and white fine art portraits from the Smithsonian Institution's National Portrait Gallery collection of notable Americans. Portraits date from the late 16th century through present day.

Notable Americans — The National Portrait Gallery. *Producer:* Abt Books, Inc.; *Operating System:* PC; *Subject:* Art; *Price:* $500; *Grade Level:* JH, HS; *Hardware:* IBM PC or compatible; 640K RAM; CD-ROM drive; VGA monitor and graphics cards; *Software:* PC-DOS or MS-DOS, Microsoft CD-ROM extensions; *Distributor:* EBSCO.

This is the first edition of the CD-ROM of the National Portrait Gallery Permanent Collection of Notable Americans, and is based on the Illustrated Checklist 1987 published version.

Time Table of History: Arts & Entertainment. *Operating System:* PC/MAC; *Subject:* Social Studies; *Price:* $130; *Grade Level:* K–C; *Hardware:* See distributor; *Software:* See distributor; *Distributor:* UPDATA.

Includes over 4,200 original stories that take you from the first cave paintings to today's computerized choreography and animation. Meet artists, writers, sculptors and performers from all ages. Allows you to search within specific date ranges. Enhanced with multimedia effects: maps, museum references, pictures, quotes, portraits, documents, and musical sound bytes.

Wild Places. *Operating System:* PC/MAC/MPC; *Subject:* Art, Music; *Price:* $29.95; *Grade Level:* General; *Hardware:* See distributor; *Software:* See distributor; *Distributor:* New Media Source.

The wilderness comes alive with over 100 striking natural landscapes and close-ups featuring deserts, rocks, seascapes, and forests. Fifty recordings of modern electronic music composed by Joyce Imbesi.

AUDIO-VISUAL

Footage '91. *Operating System:* MAC. *Subject:* Films/Videos; *Price:* $199.95; *Grade Level:* JH, HS; *Hardware:* Mac Plus/SE/II, 1MB RAM; *Software:* HyperCard 2.0; *Distributor:* UPDATA.

Search through the descriptions of over 100,000 films, videotapes, and stock shots with descriptions of more than 1600 organizations, television stations, commercial and private film archives, and university collections. Entries cover address, contact person, telephone number, collection descriptions, policy fees, and viewing and duplication facilities.

Variety's Video Directory Plus. *Producer:* Bowker; *Operating System:* PC; *Subject:* Reference; *Price:* $189 ($389 Sub-Quarterly Update); *Grade Level:* General; *Hardware:* See distributor; *Software:* See distributor; *Distributor:* CDiscovery.

Information on more than 70,000 videos, theatrical releases, educational, and documentary listings making it a valuable resource for libraries, video stores and movie buffs.

Movie Database and Software Potpourri. *Operating System:* PC; *Subject:* Entertainment; *Price:* $69; *Grade Level:* JH, HS; *Hardware:* See distributor; *Software:* See distributor; *Distributor:* Bureau of Electronic Publishing.

With 1,000 film movie database, the full text of the Bible, and hundreds of useful shareware and public domain programs (about 4,000 separate files!), this disk is probably the best single value among inexpensive CD-ROMs. In addition, the disk is equipped with an easy-to-use interface so you can quickly access the resources on the disk.

Magill's Survey of Cinema CD-ROM. *Producer:* EBSCO; *Operating System:* PC; *Subject:* Motion Pictures; *Price:* See distributor; *Grade Level:* General; *Hardware:* IBM PC, XT, or compatible; 640K RAM; 5MB hard disk space available; CD-ROM player with interface card and cable; one double-sided drive; monitor; *Software:* MS-DOS 3.2 or higher; Microsoft MS-DOS CD-ROM extensions version 2.1; *Distributor:* EBSCO.

Provides full text reviews and storyline summaries of more than 3,500 classic and contemporary films. Corresponds with Magill's cinema publications in print.

BUSINESS

The American Business Phone Book. *Operating System:* PC; *Subject:* Reference; *Price:* $99.95; *Grade Level:* General; *Hardware:* See distributor; *Software:* See distributor; *Distributor:* New Media Source.

A complete directory of every business in the U.S. — 9.2 million listings from over 5,000 Yellow Page directories.

Mavis Beacon Teaches Typing. *Operating System:* PC; *Subject:* Typing; *Price:* $99; *Grade Level:* General; *Hardware:* See distributor; *Software:* See distributor; *Distributor:* CDiscovery.

Improve productivity and learn proper keyboarding techniques with this award winning software.

Microsoft Office. *Operating System:* MAC; *Subject:* Business; *Price:* $495; *Grade Level:* JH, HS; *Hardware:* See distributor; *Software:* See distributor; *Distributor:* Bureau of Electronic Publishing.

The Microsoft Office includes four of the most successful Macintosh programs on one CD-ROM disc and now features new versions on Microsoft Excel and Microsoft Mail. Use Microsoft Word to write memos and reports, Microsoft Excel to crunch numbers and create annual-report-quality graphics; Microsoft PowerPoint to create impressive presentations; and Microsoft Mail to share information instantly. Each is a top-selling program in its own right – but when used together, they maximize the productivity of your entire office.

Microsoft Small Business Consultant. *Operating System:* PC; *Subject:* Business; *Price:* $118; *Grade Level:* General; *Hardware:* See distributor; *Software:* See distributor; *Distributor:* Bureau of Electronic Publishing.
Microsoft Small Business Consultant will give you the information you need to start, finance, and manage a small business. It's a complete library of more than 220 publications from the Small Business administration, other government agencies, and one of the country's leading accounting firms, Deloitte, Haskins & Sells.

Microsoft Stat Pack. *Operating System:* PC; *Subject:* Business; *Price:* $118; *Grade Level:* JH, HS, C; *Hardware:* See distributor; *Software:* See distributor; *Distributor:* Bureau of Electronic Publishing.
Microsoft Stat Pack is an easy, cost-effective way to get business research information you need. It provides instant access to statistical facts and figures collected by the U.S. government about people, manufacturing, industry, trade, agriculture, and business.

Money, Money, Money! *Operating System:* MAC; *Subjects:* Business/Education; *Price:* $29; *Grade Level:* General; *Hardware:* See distributor; *Software:* See distributor; *Distributor:* CD-ROM Inc.
U.S. and international coins and currency, along with 25 MPC videos of money, hot off the press. Audio tracks and sound effects make this good technology for schools and libraries.

Speed Dial. *Operating System:* PC; *Subject:* Business Telephone Numbers; *Price:* $399; *Grade Level:* General; *Hardware:* IBM PC/Compatible; *Software:* See distributor; *Distributor:* Bureau of Electronic Publishing.
Cost (2051) – PC $399; network version 2-8 users, (2051ns) $2,249; network version 9-100 users (2051nl) $2,799. Instant access to over 9.2 million business telephone numbers across the country by business name and or Yellow Page heading.

Time Table of Business, Politics & the Media. *Operating System:* MAC; *Subject:* Social Studies/Bus.; *Price:* $130; *Grade Level:* K–C; *Hardware:* IBM PC; *Software:* See distributor; *Distributor:* CDiscovery.

Includes over 6,000 stories covering the key events in the quest for wealth, power, and knowledge, from the Trojan Horse to the early stages of the Persian Gulf conflict. Additionally, stories are enhanced with multimedia effects: maps, pictures, quotes, graphs, etc.

CAREERS

Career Opportunities. Producer: Quanta Press; *Operating System:* PC; *Subject:* Careers/Employment; *Price:* $136.50; *Grade Level:* JH, HS; *Hardware:* IBM PC or compatible, 640K RAM; CD-ROM player, monitor, printer for text, one floppy disc drive; hard disk recommended; *Software:* PC-DOS or MS-DOS 2.1 or higher Microsoft CD-ROM extensions; *Distributor:* EBSCO.

This disc can help individuals and students make career choices. Included are job titles, job descriptions, education levels, chances for advancement, average salaries, and working conditions.

Improving Your Job and Career Prospects. Producer: Queue; *Operating System:* MAC/PC; *Subject:* Careers; *Price:* $145; *Grade Level:* HS, C; *Hardware:* See distributor; *Software:* See distributor; *Distributor:* CDiscovery.

Access best-selling career preparation programs to evaluate abilities, values, and goals. Learn winning interview behavior and develop effective communication skills. The contents include: Exploring Career Options, Vocabulary for the World of Work, Work and Career Options, and Business Math.

Jones in the Fast Lane. Producer: Sierra; *Operating System:* PC; *Subjects:* Careers/Guidance; *Price:* $60; *Grade Level:* General; *Hardware:* See distributor; *Software:* See distributor; *Distributor:* CDiscovery.

Hours of fun when players reach their goals of economics, happiness, education, and careers.

Peterson's College Database. Producer: SilverPlatter Information, Inc. *Operating System:* PC/MAC; *Subject:* Colleges/Reference; *Price:* $595; *Grade Level:* JH, HS, C; *Hardware:* See distributor; *Software:* See distributor; *Distributor:* EBSCO.

Individual descriptive profiles of 3,300 accredited degree-granting colleges in the U.S. and Canada. Expenses, financial aid, board score ranges, housing, athletics, majors offered, and ethnic/geographic statistics.

COMPUTERS

BMUG CD ROM. *Producer:* Discovery Systems; *Operating System:* MAC; *Subject:* Entertainment, Education; *Price:* $99.95; *Grade Level:* General; *Hardware:* See distributor; *Software:* See distributor; *Distributor:* CDiscovery.

Public domain software that contains over 500+ games, 300+ educational programs, 1,000 hyperstack cards, 1,000 pictures, 100 F Keys, 200+ telecom programs, 250 desk accessories, 800 fonts, 200 graphics packages, 300+ MAC II programs, 600+ utilities, 500+ programming tools, 100 sounds, and 200 utilities.

Bibliofile/Software Support. *Producer:* The Library Corporation; *Operating System:* PC; *Subject:* Software Support; *Price:* $420; *Hardware:* Annual Software support from the Library Corporation; *Distributor:* EBSCO.

Annual software support fee. For the complete system, continuation of first year's software enhancements service and customer support from the Library Corporation.

ClubMac. *Operating System:* MAC; *Subject:* Shareware; *Price:* $129; *Grade Level:* General; *Hardware:* See distributor; *Software:* See distributor; *Distributor:* Bureau of Electronic Publishing.

ClubMac contains a highly organized collection of Apple Macintosh public domain, shareware, and demoware programs, with retrieval through HyperCard. Highly descriptive information about each file.

Computer Library. *Producer:* SilverPlatter; *Operating System:* PC/MAC; *Subject:* Computers; *Price:* $450; *Grade Level:* JH, HS, C; *Hardware:* See distributor; *Software:* See distributor; *Distributor:* UPDATA.

Information on every aspect of computers. Over 270,000 records on computer related literature cover the subject from the earliest days of computer development to the microchip revolution. Almost half of the records are on material published after 1980. Topics include computer applications, mathmatical applications, and electronic communications.

MacGUIDE. *Operating System:* Mac; *Subject:* Computer products; *Price:* $29; *Grade Level:* General; *Hardware:* See distributor; *Software:* See distributor; *Distributor:* Bureau of Electronic Publishing.

Listings of over 4,000 products for use with Apple Macintosh computers. Also containing approximately 1,000 product reviews, demonstrations of more than 300 popular software packages, and approximately 450mb of shareware and public domain software of use on the Macintosh. Each product listing contains a description along with the price, version, manufacturer information, and more.

Mac Buyer's Guide. *Operating System:* MAC; *Subject:* Reference; *Price:* $149; *Grade Level:* General; *Hardware:* See distributor; *Software:* See distributor; *Distributor:* CDiscovery.

Source for thousands of Macintosh and Apple IIGS products. Includes all software, hardware, and accessories. Complete with description, system requirements, name, address, and phone number of the supplier and prices.

MicroSoft Bookshelf. *Operating System:* PC/MAC; *Subject:* Reference; *Price:* $189; *Grade Level:* General; *Hardware:* See distributor; *Software:* See distributor; *Distributor:* Bureau of Electronic Publishing.

For users who do not have Windows 3.0, the DOS version of Bookshelf has been updated for the '90s. This character-based core reference set for home, office, or school puts the facts and figures of an entire reference library on your PC. Pick a topic and browse whole volumes with a few simple keystrokes. Or incorporate text from the Bookshelf library into your word processing documents in seconds.

Window Book Library. *Operating System:* PC; *Subject:* Reference; *Price:* $99; *Grade Level:* General; *Hardware:* See distributor; *Software:* See distributor; *Distributor:* UPDATA.

A potpourri of computer language tutors, designed for those who want to get more out of DOS; those interested in programming with ADA, AWK, and RTF; those seeking information about items as diverse as astronomy, the United States Postal Service regulations, GSA regulations, and PC functions and text conversions.

All of MacTutor. *Producer:* Wayzata Tech; *Operating System:* MAC; *Subject:* Computer Lit.; *Price:* $199; *Grade Level:* HS; *Hardware:* See distributor; *Software:* See distributor; *Distributor:* CDiscovery.

Information from all the "MacTutor" issues from 12/84 to 12/89, every article, editorial, source code, and letter.

CD-Rom Directory. *Producer:* Unidisc; *Operating System:* PC; *Subject:* Reference; *Price:* $149; *Grade Level:* General; *Hardware:* See distributor; *Software:* See distributor; *Distributor:* Bureau of Electronic Publishing.

Catalog of commercially available CD-ROM software including description of each title in outline form and simulation of the product provided by the publisher.

CD-ROM Sourcedisc. *Producer:* Diversified Data Resources; *Operating System:* PC; *Subject:* Software; *Price:* $90; *Grade Level:* JH, HS; *Hardware:* See distributor; *Software:* See distributor; *Distributor:* CDiscovery.

Catalog of commercially available CD-ROM software including description of each title in outline form and simulation of the product provided by the publisher.

Educorp CD-ROM Software Library. *Producer:* Educorp Computer Services; *Operating System:* MAC; *Subject:* Software; *Price:* $203; *Grade Level:* General; *Hardware:* Macintosh Plus or higher/20MB Hard disk: 2MB RAM; CD-ROM player; *Software:* See distributor; *Distributor:* EBSCO.

The complete Educorp software library including over 10,000 different files (over 625 megabytes) of public domain software. It includes laser quality clip art, educational software for all ages, animation, full-color graphics, desk accessories, and fonts.

Shareware Gold. *Producer:* Quanta Press; *Operating System:* PC; *Subject:* Shareware; *Price:* $136.50; *Grade Level:* General; *Hardware:* See distributor; *Software:* See distributor; *Distributor:* EBSCO.

Shareware Gold is a menu driven CD-ROM that contains not only DOS programs, but also reviews of each program. This is the perfect disc for the business environment. No going through thousands of programs, EBSCO has selected the cream-of-the-crop of shareware for you. Each and every shareware program has been verified virus-free.

Shareware Gold II. *Producer:* Sherburne Knowledge Systems, Inc.; *Operating System:* PC; *Subject:* Shareware; *Price:* $138; *Grade Level:* General; *Hardware:* See distributor; *Software:* See distributor; *Distributor:* EBSCO.

Contains 250 of the very best shareware programs available. Each program is categorized and reviewed to save the user time and effort in selecting the appropriate program.

Shareware Express. *Operating System:* PC/MAC; *Subject:* Shareware; *Price:* $49; *Grade Level:* General; *Hardware:* See distributor; *Software:* See distributor; *Distributor:* Bureau of Electronic Publishing.

Contains a wealth of useful software with business, educational, recreational, and programming applications.

Shareware Grab-bag. *Operating System:* PC; *Subject:* Shareware; *Price:* $88; *Grade Level:* General; *Hardware:* See distributor; *Software:* See distributor; *Distributor:* Bureau of Electronic Publishing.

This disc contains 7,000 different software programs with the wide range of application and utility areas, including line and text editing, data communications, personal and business finance, hard disk utilities, graphics, device drivers, educational programs, and others.

Software DuJour. *Producer:* Varied; *Operating System:* PC; *Subject:* Computer Programs Public Domain; *Price:* $49.95; *Grade Level:* General; *Hardware:* IBM PC/Compatible; *Software:* See distributor; *Distributor:* UPDATA.

Software for education, business, recreation, and programming.

PC-SIG Library. *Producer:* PC-SIG, Inc. *Operating System:* PC; *Subject:* Software Programs; *Price:* $500; *Grade Level:* General; *Hardware:* IBM PC XT, AT or compatible; 256K RAM (384 K to use Wordcruncher); CD-ROM player; *Software:* PC-DOS or MS-DOS 3.1 or higher, Microsoft CD-ROM extensions; *Distributor:* EBSCO.

This database includes over 1,200 software titles and thousands of software programs for the IBM PC and compatibles; completely menu driven format. WordCruncher text retrieval system; Shareware and public domain software. Some software categories are accounting, children and education, CAD, religion, reference, spreadsheets, science, mathematics, teaching, and word processing.

Grips 2 CD-ROM. *Operating System:* PC/MAC; *Subject:* Shareware/ maps; *Price:* $49; *Grade Level:* General; *Hardware:* See distributor; *Software:* See distributor; *Distributor:* Bureau of Electronic Publishing.

Contains a wide variety of high resolution images and fractual images. Public domain can be incorporated into your own presentations.

Study Room. *Operating System:* PC; *Subject:* Educational Shareware, Public Domain; *Price:* $30; *Grade Level:* JH, HS, C; *Hardware:* Macintosh; *Software:* See distributor; *Distributor:* Ztek.

Educational public domain and shareware.

CURRENT EVENTS

Boston Globe (Current Year + 1 year Backfile). *Producer:* DIALOG Information Services; *Operating System:* PC; *Subject:* Reference; *Price:* $2,025; *Grade Level:* JH, HS, C; *Hardware:* IBM PC or compatible; 640K RAM; 10MB hard disk recommended; CD-ROM player; printer optional; *Software:* PC-DOS or MS-DOS 3.1 or higher. Microsoft CD-ROM extensions; *Distributor:* EBSCO.

Contains the complete text of all staff-written news stories, features, columns, and editorials published in the *Boston Globe,* the largest source of information from the American northeast. A general circulation newspaper providing local and national coverage. Also covered are science, real estate, the arts, entertainment, and sports.

Facts on File News Digest CD-ROM. *Producer:* Facts on File, Inc.; *Operating System:* PC/MAC; *Subject:* Reference/News; *Price:* $795; *Grade Level:* JH, HS, C; *Hardware:* See distributor; *Software:* See distributor; *Distributor:* EBSCO.

This database contains all information published in the print version of the *News Digest,* a fully indexed, weekly compilation of national and foreign news from leading American and international sources, from 1980 to 1990. Over 9,000 pages of text and 12 million words can be accessed using full text Boolean searching. Also includes over 500 maps.

Front Page News. *Producer:* Buckmaster Publishing; *Operating System:* PC; *Subject:* Current Events; *Price:* $149; *Grade Level:* JH, HS; *Hardware:* IBM PC, XT, AT, PS/2, 386 or compatible with 640K RAM; hard disk; *Software:* MS/PC-DOS 3.1 or higher; *Distributor:* UPDATA.

Provides world-wide news coverage from over 15 American and international news sources and wire services. Contains more than 200,000 articles varying in length with a variety of viewpoints.

Magazine Rack. *Operating System:* PC; *Subject:* Business; *Price:* $89; *Grade Level:* General; *Hardware:* See distributor; *Software:* See distributor; *Distributor:* Bureau of Electronic Publishing.

Magazine Rack is a tool with hundreds of uses. Use the rack to get background on current events or to scope out the best buys in 35mm cameras. Use it to gather data for business presentations or to satisfy curiosity. Informational tool.

Social Science Source CD-ROM. Producer: EBSCO. *Operating System:* PC; *Subject:* Reference; *Price:* See distributor; *Grade Level:* General; *Hardware:* IBM PC, XT, or compatible, 640K RAM; 5MB hard disk space available; CD-ROM player with interface card and cable; one double-sided drive; monitor; *Software:* MS-DOS 3.2 or higher; Microsoft MS-DOS CD-ROM extensions version 2.1; *Distributor:* EBSCO.

Provides broad-based, comprehensive abstract and index coverage of 353 journals in economics, political science, public policy, international relations, psychology, and sociology. Searchable full text is included for approximately 15 of these journals.

Washington Times and Insight on the News. Operating System: PC/MAC; *Subject:* Reference; *Price:* $149; *Grade Level:* General; *Hardware:* See distributor; *Software:* See distributor; *Distributor:* UPDATA.

Combines news with editorial insights for a deeper understanding of today's events.

SIRS-CD-ROM. Producer: Social Issues Resources Series, Inc.; *Operating System:* PC; *Subject:* Science, Social Science; *Price:* See distributor. Cost depends on programs; *Grade Level:* HS, C; *Hardware:* See distributor; *Software:* See distributor; *Distributor:* Social Issues Resources Series, Inc.

Thousands of full-text articles from newspapers, magazines and government documents covering important events and enduring issues in the sciences and social sciences. Complete bibliographic citations included.

Time Magazine Compact Almanac. Operating System: PC; *Subject:* Reference; *Price:* $195 Proprietary; $149 Annual Update; *Grade Level:* General; *Hardware:* IBM PC; *Software:* See distributor; *Distributor:* Ztek.

Nearly 5,000 articles including the full text of *Time* magazine from 1989 to date, as well as articles on major stories and events from 1923 to 1988. Statistical abstracts, full color maps of the world, complete congressional directory (with fax and phone numbers). School edition includes 32-page user's guide and new teacher's guide. Motion video and sound from CNN highlight the Gulf War, the Berlin Wall, Tiananmen Square and 25 other events from 1989 to 1991.

DICTIONARIES

Dictionary of the Living World. Producer: Ztek; *Operating System:* MAC; *Subject:* Biology; *Price:* $395; *Grade Level:* JH, HS; *Hardware:* At least 2MB RAM; *Software:* Hypercard 2.0; *Distributor:* Ztek.

Database containing 3,000 text entries, 500 color photos, and sounds. Also includes a biological dictionary for students.

Macmillan Dictionary for Children. *Producer:* Macmillan; *Operating System:* MPC; *Subject:* Reference; *Price:* $44.95; *Grade Level:* K, Elem.; *Hardware:* See distributor; *Software:* See distributor; *Distributor:* New Media Source.

The Macmillan Dictionary for Children employs the power of multimedia to assemble 12,000 word entries, 1,000 illustrations and 400 sound effects into a learning experience that's a lot of fun.

Officer's Bookcase—Terms. *Producer:* Quanta Press; *Operating System:* PC; *Subject:* Government; *Grade Level:* JH, HS; *Hardware:* IBM PC, XT, AT or compatible; printer for text (optional); CD player with card, cable; *Software:* PC-DOS or MS-DOS 2.1 or higher, Microsoft CD-ROM extensions; *Distributor:* EBSCO.

The definitive CD-ROM disc for military terms and acronyms. The disc contains the Joint Chiefs of Staff "Military Terms Dictionary," the "Defense Acquisition Acronyms and Terms" and the Soviet Thought Series volume "Soviet Terms Dictionary." The disc utilizes a customized version of the list program for easy access to hundreds of terms and acronyms.

Oxford English Dictionary on CD-ROM. *Producer:* Oxford University Press; *Operating System:* PC; *Subject:* Reference; *Price:* $965; *Grade Level:* JH, HS, C; *Hardware:* IBM PC or compatible, 640K RAM; hard disk; CD-ROM drive; *Software:* PC-DOS or MS-DOS, Microsoft CD-ROM extensions; *Distributor:* EBSCO.

Contains all of the original 12-volume set of the Oxford English Dictionary. Usage and etymology covers the entire vocabulary from the Middle Ages to the twentieth century.

Webster's Talking Dictionary. *Operating System:* MAC. *Subject:* Reference; *Price:* $175; *Grade Level:* General; *Hardware:* See distributor; *Software:* See distributor; *Distributor:* UPDATA.

Learn to correctly pronounce any word in English by hearing it spoken. There are 160,000 entries and 200,000 definitions. This computer edition allows a user to point a mouse and verify spelling and pronunciation at the same time, while the monitor also displays the word meaning, making it ideal for use by school libraries, English classes, and anyone who needs to speak publicly.

Zyzomys. Operating System: PC; *Subject:* French; *Price:* $495; *Grade Level:* HS, C; *Hardware:* See distributor; *Software:* See distributor; *Distributor:* CDiscovery.

Data from the *Dictionnaire de Notre Temps, Dictionnaire des Synonymes,* and the *Atlas Pratique.* Also includes conjugation of verbs, practical grammar rules, and letter writing conventions.

Findit Webster. *Producer:* Innotech, Inc.; *Operating System:* PC/MAC; *Subject:* Reference/Dictionary; *Price:* $104; *Grade Level:* JH, HS, C; *Hardware:* See distributor; *Software:* See distributor; *Distributor:* EBSCO.

This disc contains over 85,000 entries with sub-entries of words logically grouped to reduce confusion and speed up the time needed for word and idea searching. Contains the full text of the original *New York Times Everyday Dictionary.*

EDUCATION

Alliance Plus. *Producer:* Follett; *Operating System:* PC; *Subject:* Education; *Price:* $950; *Grade Level:* General; *Hardware:* IBM PC or compatible; 640K RAM; *Software:* PC-DOS or MS-DOS, Microsoft CD-ROM extensions; *Distributor:* EBSCO.

Contains more than 300,000 book, audio-visual, serial, and juvenile records, many of which have been enhanced for the school marketplace. Allows you to perform your own shelflist retrospective conversion efficiently and painlessly. In addition, quarterly updates will provide high-quality records for new acquisitions. Alliance Plus is the only LC MARC CD-ROM product on the market which has direct interface with Circulation/Catalog Plus.

Educational Games for Young Children. *Operating System:* MAC; *Subject:* Education/Entertainment; *Price:* $95; *Grade Level:* K, Elem.; *Hardware:* See distributor; *Software:* See distributor; *Distributor:* CDiscovery.

A collection of seven best-selling programs for the development of early skills. Titles include The Boars Tell Time, Early Games for Young Children, How Many?, Easy as ABC, Not Like the Others, What Comes Next?

The International Encyclopedia of Education. *Producer:* Pergamon Compact Solution; *Operating System:* PC; *Subject:* Reference; *Price:* $2,150; *Grade Level:* General; *Hardware:* IBM PC or compatible; 640K

RAM hard disk; CD-ROM player; printer for text; monitor – Hercules EGA or VGA with card; *Software:*PC-DOS or MS-DOS 3.1 or higher, Microsoft CD-ROM extensions; *Distributor:* EBSCO.

Contains 1,448 descriptive and analytical articles covering all aspects of educational research from the theory and economics of education to vocational training techniques. Many of the articles are accompanied by tables, graphs and charts which help to provide useful insights into the subject matter.

ERIC. *Producer:* SilverPlatter Information, Inc.; *Operating System:* PC/MAC; *Subject:* Reference/Education; *Price:* $650; *Grade Level:* General; *Hardware:* See distributor; *Software:* See distributor; *Distributor:* EBSCO.

A bibliographic database covering the journal and technical literature in the field of education, ERIC is compiled by the ERIC Processing and Reference Facility. The ERIC database consists of Resources in Education (RIE), covering the fugitive document literature, and Current Index to Journals in Education (CIJE), covering the published journal literature from over 775 periodicals. Current disc covers 1983 to the present and the Archival disc set covers 1966–1982. Subscription includes tutorial/thesaurus.

R3. *Operating System:* MAC; *Subject:* Education; *Price:* $30; *Grade Level:* JH, HS; *Hardware:* See distributor; *Software:* See distributor; *Distributor:* Ztek.

The three Rs are all here on this disc of educational public domain and shareware (subset of Class Room CD-ROM).

ENCYCLOPEDIAS

Compton's Family Encyclopedia. *Producer:* Britannica; *Operating System:* PC/MAC; *Subject:* Reference; *Price:* $695; *Grade Level:* JH, HS, C; *Hardware:* See distributor; *Software:* See distributor; *Distributor:* CDiscovery.

The 26 volumes of the 1992 print edition of *Compton's Encyclopedia,* with its eight million words in over 3,000 articles, 15,000 images, maps and graphs, 30 minutes of sound, and an interactive, multiple window World Atlas. The program contains five entry paths, the *Complete Webster's Intermediate Dictionary,* a spell-checker, a research path, an electronic bookmark, and a notebook which allows users to cut, paste, and write their own notes. On some subjects, there are not only pictures but sound (such as a Mozart composition accompanying the Mozart text entry). Users can type in questions and find the answers immediately.

Compton's Multimedia Encyclopedia. *Producer:* Britannica; *Operating System:* PC/MPC; *Subject:* Reference; *Price:* $795/$895; *Grade Level:* JH, HS, C; *Hardware:* See distributor; *Software:* See distributor; *Distributor:* Bureau of Electronic Publishing.

A multi-media encyclopedia with mouse-driven commands, utilizes full text, pictures, sound, animation, and an on-line dictionary. Contains the full text of 31,200 articles containing 8.7 million words, 60 minutes of sound, 10,000 photographs, 5,800 maps, charts and graphs, eight multiple entry paths, and an audio glossary with 1,500 words. Features: U.S. History Timeline, Scientific Feature Articles, Title Finder, and On-line Notepad. Special features, such as Take Another Look which helps students to grasp hard-to-understand concepts.

The Grolier Electronic Encyclopedia. *Producer:* Grolier Electronic Publishing; *Operating System:* PC/MAC; *Subject:* Reference; *Price:* $395; *Grade Level:* Elem., JH, HS; *Hardware:* See distributor; *Software:* See distributor; *Distributor:* EBSCO.

This version includes 33,000 articles (10 million words), nearly 4,000 new or revised articles and thousands of pictures in full color, 250 high-resolution color maps, CD-quality audio that includes excerpts from famous speeches—musical compositions, animal sounds, and more. Also features Boolean search capabilities, "notepads" and electronic bookmarks to save, cut, paste and retrieve stored information, "links" for cross-referencing, and more.

The Hutchinson Encyclopedia. *Operating System:* PC; *Subject:* Reference; *Price:* $200; *Grade Level:* JH, HS; *Hardware:* See distributor; *Software:* See distributor; *Distributor:* UPDATA.

First published in 1948, the *Hutchinson Encyclopedia* is the longest established and best-selling single volume encyclopedia in the United Kingdom. This latest edition (9th) is in full color and contains over 25,000 entries (including 2,000 new entries), 2,500 illustrations, 50 color maps integrated with the text, and tables of facts and figures. Also features the International Phonetic Alphabet with 11,000 pronunciations for every person and place. Over 1,500,000 words and 7,500 biographies.

Toolworks '92 Encyclopedia. *Operating System:* PC/MAC; *Subject:* Reference; *Price:* $395; *Grade Level:* P–C; *Hardware:* IBM PC/MAC; *Software:* See distributor; *Distributor:* CDiscovery.

Illustrated encyclopedia updated for 1992.

ENTERTAINMENT

Between Heaven and Hell II. *Producer:* Bureau of Electronic Publishing, Inc.; *Operating System:* PC; *Subject:* Entertainment; *Price:* $104; *Grade Level:* General; *Hardware:* IBM PC, XT, AT PS/2 or compatible; 640 K RAM; monochrome, VGA card; CD-ROM drive (ISO 9660 standards); fixed disk suggested; *Software:* DOS 3.1 or higher; Microsoft extensions 2.0 or higher; *Distributor:* EBSCO.

A public domain software disc for the PC user. It contains dozens of games, broad selection of graphic images, full text of the Bible, chemistry tutors, calorie counters, a federal building life-cycle cost calculator. There are also hundreds of programs you would expect on a complete shareware collection, including extended disk managers, JIVE, DOG disk organizer, PKZIP, DEGRAG, etc. for a total of 12,109 files on the disc.

CD Fun House. *Producer:* Wayzata; *Operating System:* MAC; *Subject:* Games/Entertainment; *Price:* $38; *Grade Level:* JH, HS; *Hardware:* See distributor; *Software:* See distributor; *Distributor:* Bureau of Electronic Publishing.

A database of over 50MB of games and entertainment software that includes hours of fun and many popular titles: Adventureland, Games Parlour, Word Games, Sports Palace, Star Fleet HQ, the Simulator, the Arcade, the Casino, the School House.

Manhole. *Operating System:* MAC; *Subject:* Entertainment; *Price:* $49; *Grade Level:* General; *Hardware:* See distributor; *Software:* See distributor; *Distributor:* Bureau of Electronic Publishing.

A journey to fantasy and wonder for kids of all ages. Unusual entertainment software for the Mac.

GEOGRAPHY

Aloha, Hawaii. *Operating System:* PC; *Subject:* Geography/Travel; *Price:* $39; *Grade Level:* JH, HS; *Hardware:* See distributor; *Software:* See distributor; *Distributor:* Bureau of Electronic Publishing.

This educational and entertaining exploration is made available through an easy, intuitive map and icon interface. Focusing on the main island of Hawaii, the viewer has only to click on the pictorial buttons and mapped areas to access animations, facts, and "inside knowledge." Contains CD-quality sounds and over 2,000 color photos of this locale's unique East-West culture. For travelers, students, educators, and artists alike.

Atlas Pack. *Operating System:* PC; *Subject:* Geography; *Price:* $109; *Grade Level:* JH, HS; *Hardware:* See distributor; *Software:* See distributor; *Distributor:* UPDATA.

The Atlas Pack is a comprehensive reference work that is an excellent research tool for libraries, businesses, students, travelers, and home users. It contains 238 high quality, full-color maps. There are maps of every country and world statistics maps. The accompanying text is under five different subject areas: geography, people, government, economy, and communications. Data sets for statistical maps can be accessed in alphabetical order, by country or numerical order of data. Reports including maps and text can be printed using Epson or Hewlett-Packard LaserJet Printers and text can be printed using any printer. The program operates with a mouse or keyboard. The point-and-click graphic interface is easy to use, powerful and flexible. Country maps may be retrieved by pointing to them on an index map. The United States and state data with 200 topics as well as statistics on ten subjects and city information on 160 cities with 20 different areas of information are covered. Reference maps of 50 states and Washington, D.C., display cities, highways, adjoining states, and bodies of water. Both maps and text files can be exported to disc in various formats (.PCX, TIFF, ASCII, etc.) for use in desktop publishing or word processing.

Countries of the World. *Producer:* Bureau of Electronic Printing; *Operating System:* PC/MAC; *Subject:* Reference; *Price:* $395; *Grade Level:* General; *Hardware:* See distributor; *Software:* See distributor; *Distributor:* Bureau of Electronic Publishing.

Countries of the World contains the full text of over 100 country references, featuring thousands of color and black and white maps, images, and tables. Based on the U.S. Army's popular *Area Handbook Series* this CD-ROM provides extremely detailed coverage of every country in the world. Topics covered for each country include the historical setting, society, environment, economy, government, politics, and national security.

Electronic Map Cabinet. *Producer:* Highlighted Data, Inc.; *Operating System:* MAC; *Subject:* Geography; *Price:* $199.95; *Grade Level:* General; *Hardware:* Macintosh 1MB RAM CD-ROM Drive; *Software:* See distributor; *Distributor:* EBSCO.

This product is a tool for constructing detailed maps of the U.S. or any region of the U.S., at the scale and level of detail specified by the teachers or students. Level of detail is controlled by choosing options such as international, state, county, and city boundaries, coastal and inland waters, major interstate highways, ferries and tunnels, railroads and airports, five different city population ranges. National parks, monuments, forests, Indian reservations, and military bases can be shown.

Exotic Japan. Operating System: MAC; *Subject:* Japan/Geography; *Price:* $79; *Grade Level:* General; *Hardware:* Macintosh Plus; *Software:* HyperCard or SuperCard; *Distributor:* EBSCO.

A multimedia exploration of the country, its people, language, culture, and music. Disc features a new look at modern society, home living, business practices, greetings, geography, and traveling tips. Includes over 1,600 specially-recorded native language and music sounds.

Geodisc U.S. Atlas. Producer: GeoVision, Inc.; *Operating System:* PC; *Subject:* Geography; *Price:* $495; *Grade Level:* JH, HS, C; *Hardware:* IBM PC or compatible; 640K RAM; 10MB hard disk; CD-ROM player; EGA, VGA or equivalent graphics card and monitor; *Software:* PC-DOS or MS-DOS 3.2 or higher, Microsoft CD-ROM extensions; *Distributor:* EBSCO.

This is a geographic database containing a complete digital representation of the U.S. at the 1:2,000,000 scale. It includes major highways, waterways, political boundaries, railroads, federal land areas, and hydrological districts. Also contained is a complete place and landmark names file of more than 1,000,000 entries.

Great Cities of the World. Operating System: PC/MAC; *Subject:* Geography/Travel; *Price:* $129; *Grade Level:* JH, HS, C; *Hardware:* See distributor; *Software:* See distributor; *Distributor:* CDiscovery.

A travel guide depicting the ten most intriguing cities of the world including Bombay, Cairo, Los Angeles, Moscow, New York, Paris, Rio de Janeiro, Sydney, and Tokyo plus a detailed history of each city with narrative and local music, and recordings of useful phrases.

Hawaii. Producer: Motherlode; *Operating System:* PC; *Subject:* Geography/Travel; *Price:* $129; *Grade Level:* Elem., JH, HS; *Hardware:* See distributor; *Software:* See distributor; *Distributor:* CDiscovery.

A multimedia excursion through our fiftieth state. View the main island of Hawaii by clicking on the pictorial buttons and mapped areas to access animations, facts through CD-quality music and sounds plus 1,500 color photo-shows.

The Orient. *Operating System:* MAC; *Subject:* Geography; *Price:* $99; *Grade Level:* JH, HS; *Hardware:* See distributor; *Software:* See distributor; *Distributor:* Bureau of Electronic Publishing.

The Orient, volume 1 of the Interactive Travel Encyclopedia, covers the region's 16 countries and 42 major cities. The 16 countries included are Brunei, Cambodia, China, Hong Kong, Indonesia, Japan, Laos, Macau, Malaysia, North Korea, Philippines, Singapore, South Korea, Taiwan, Thailand, and Vietnam.

Sophisticated Santa Fe. *Operating System:* PC; *Subject:* Santa Fe, New Mexico; *Price:* $59; *Grade Level:* K–C; *Hardware:* IBM PC 640 RAM Mouse, Dos 3.0; *Software:* Search Software Proprietary; *Distributor:* UPDATA.

A festive and factual visual guide that explores the sights, symbols, and flavor of being in a millennium-old American location, Santa Fe, New Mexico. The oldest historic territory in the United States, Santa Fe combines a unique blend of traditions and cosmopolitan life. The data and images are made accessible through an intuitive interface; clicking on pictorial buttons enables the user to access the more than 1,500 full-color photos and the 36 categories which range from sports to sacred arts. The disc contains 120 slide-show vignettes about the city.

SuperMap. *Operating System:* PC; *Subject:* Reference; *Price:* $990 County level; $799 County level – PC; $2,240 Tract Level (1 region) – PC; $2,300 Tract Level (2 regions) – PC; $2,350 (Tract Level) (3 regions) – PC; $2,400 Tract Level (4 regions) – PC; *Grade Level:* General; *Hardware:* IBM PC; *Software:* See distributor; *Distributor:* Bureau of Electronic Publishing.

Access 1980 U.S. Census data and matching digital mapping data displayed in various colors.

Time Traveler. *Operating System:* MAC; *Subject:* Geography; *Price:* $99.95; *Grade Level:* Elem.–C; *Hardware:* Macintosh; *Software:* See distributor; *Distributor:* New Media Source.

Travel through any period of history from 4000 B.C. to the present. Five geographical regions can be explored – the Americas, Africa, Asia, the Middle East, and Europe.

U.S. Atlas. *Operating System:* PC; *Subject:* Geography; *Price:* $79; *Grade Level:* General; *Hardware:* See distributor; *Software:* See distributor; *Distributor:* UPDATA.

Factual information about all 50 states. Statistical information and illustrations are included.

USA STATE Factbook. Producer: Quanta Press; *Operating System:* PC/MAC; *Subject:* Reference; *Price:* $136.50; *Grade Level:* Elem.–C; *Hardware:* IBM PC compatible; *Software:* See distributor; *Distributor:* EBSCO.

An almanac of the USA and its territories. Facts, figures and historical data on such subjects as geography, people, government, economies, communications, icons, traditions, even state fungi. Line drawings of state seals and maps of the 50 states and the U.S. territories.

Where in the World Is Carmen Sandiego? Operating System: PC; *Subject:* Geography/Entertainment; *Price:* $69.95; *Grade Level:* General; *Hardware:* See distributor; *Software:* See distributor; *Distributor:* New Media Source.

Sixty countries are involved with Carmen and her gang of villains, plus ten new recruits, who are stealing treasures of the world. Clues of increasing difficulty are involved so players can learn about reference skills and geography through entertainment.

World Atlas. Operating System: PC/MPC; *Subject:* Geography; *Price:* MPC $149; PC $79; PC (Windows) $89; *Grade Level:* General; *Hardware:* See distributor; *Software:* See distributor; *Distributor:* Bureau of Electronic Publishing.

Contains over 240 full-color maps and hundreds of pages of textual information and brings a world of geographic information to your computer screen — an atlas, almanac, and world book of facts all in one. The MPC version gives you national anthems from over 200 countries and over 200 animated flags in VGA color.

GOVERNMENT

American Government. Producer: Queue; *Operating System:* MAC/PC; *Subject:* Social Studies/Government; *Price:* $295; *Grade Level:* JH, HS; *Hardware:* See distributor; *Software:* See distributor; *Distributor:* CDiscovery.

Complete introduction to American government studies. The series includes How Our Government Works (American legal and political systems in self-contained lesson modules); American Government I–IV (interactive tutorials provide students with an understanding of the developments and processes within the American governmental system); Citizenship Series (four highly interactive programs explaining rights, voting and the U.S. Government); You and the Law (complete interactive legal course introduces students to the law).

The Constitution Papers. *Operating System:* PC; *Subject:* Government/ History — Reference; *Price:* $99; *Grade Level:* JH, HS; *Hardware:* See distributor; *Software:* See distributor; *Distributor:* Bureau of Electronic Publishing.

Contains the texts of the most historic American documents (the Constitution, Washington's Farewell Address), and many of the documents that helped to shape the Constitution: Virginia Randolph Plan, The Federalist Papers, New Jersey Plan, Hamilton's Plan of the Union. There are many documents that helped shape the United States, from the writings that incited the American colonist to sever with England (*Common Sense* by Thomas Paine), to the Constitutions of the original 13 states, plus early law (Monroe Doctrine, Mayflower Compact) and more.

Government Statistics on CD-ROM. *Producer:* Bureau of Electronic Publishing; *Operating System:* PC; *Subject:* Statistics; *Price:* $1,200 — County and City Statistics; $2,200 — Business Indicators Service; *Grade Level:* General; *Hardware:* See distributor; *Software:* See distributor; *Distributor:* CDiscovery.

Complete listing of county, city and metro area statistics on subjects ranging from population to climate compiled by the Census Bureau. The disc includes three databases: County Statistics, City Statistics, Population and Income. Three complete databases consisting of: U.S. National Income and Product or GNP contains 5,000 data items related to GNP, national income, personal income, prices, personal consumption, etc.; U.S. Department of Commerce with national data covering manufacturing, wholesale and retail trade, industrial production, consumer and producer prices, employment, foreign trade, and financial indicators; Income Employment by State.

U.S. Civics. *Operating System:* PC/MAC; *Subject:* Civics; *Price:* $39.95; *Grade Level:* JH, HS; *Hardware:* See distributor; *Software:* See distributor; *Distributor:* New Media Source.

A student's and instructor's guide to U.S. civics from the 1700s to the present. Biographies, government structure reference manuals, and sample tests round out this educational database.

U.S. Civics/Citizenship Disc. *Operating System:* PC/MAC; *Subject:* Social Studies; *Price:* $124; *Grade Level:* General; *Hardware:* IBM PC/Macintosh; *Software:* See distributor; *Distributor:* UPDATA.

The U.S. Civics/Citizenship disc is designed especially for persons seeking U.S. citizenship, researching the origins of the United States or teaching American History. The database consists of the U.S. Department of Justice, Immigration and Naturalization Service's Federal Citizenship Texts. These texts include "A Reference Manual for Citizenship Instructors," "Citizenship Education and Naturalization Information," "United States History," and "U.S. Government Structure."

HEALTH

American Family Physician. Producer: CMC ReSearch, Inc.; *Operating System:* PC; *Subject:* Medicine; *Price:* $400; *Grade Level:* JH, HS, C; *Hardware:* IBM or compatible PC; hard disk; CD-ROM player with MS-CDEX; 640K RAM; Image display requires VGA video board; *Software:* PC-DOS or MS-DOS, Microsoft CD-ROM extensions; *Distributor:* EBSCO.

American Family Physician is the official clinical journal of the American Academy of Family Physicians. *AFP* provides continuing medical education for family physicians and other physicians involved in primary care. Each issue of *AFP* contains original scientific articles which emphasize diagnostic and therapeutic techniques, as well as abstracts from major medical journals and reports on recent developments in medicine. Disc covers 1985–89 with complete original full text, tables and black and white images.

Bird-CD-ROM. Producer: International Children's Center; *Operating System:* PC; *Subject:* Health/Children; *Price:* $3,200; *Grade Level:* General; *Hardware:* IBM PC or compatible; hard disk; 480K RAM; *Software:* MS-DOS 3.1 or higher; *Distributor:* EBSCO.

Database contains 100,200 references related to public health, health education, community health, nutrition, handicapped children, sociocultural environment of children, children's rights, battered children, and children in the media. Produced in France.

The Family Doctor. Producer: CMC ReSearch; *Operating System:* PC; *Subject:* Medicine; *Price:* $184; *Grade Level:* General; *Hardware:* IBM PC, AT, XT; CD-ROM player, MS-CDEX; image display requires VGA video board with 512K RAM and VGA monitor; *Software:* DOS 3.1 or higher; Microsoft CDEX extensions version 2.1 or higher; *Distributor:* EBSCO.

The Family Doctor on CD-ROM provides instant access to comprehensive and easy to understand medical information. Edited by Alan Bruckheim, M.D., FAAFP, nationally recognized physician and syndicated columnist. The disc provides invaluable home medical information in easy to understand language from multiple sources and perspectives.

Oxford Textbook of Medicine, 2nd Edition. Producer: Oxford University Press; *Operating System:* PC; *Subject:* Medicine; *Price:* $505; *Grade Level:* JH, HS, C; *Hardware:* IBM PC or compatible; 640K RAM; hard disk; CD-ROM drive; *Software:* PC-DOS, MS-DOS; *Distributor:* EBSCO.

Includes the complete text of the second edition of the *Oxford Textbook of Medicine* and five electronic indexes. Covers all areas of internal medicine, including epidemiology, diagnosis, clinical details, treatment, and side effects.

Nursing and Allied Health. Producer: SilverPlatter Information, Inc.; *Operating System:* PC/MAC; *Subject:* Nursing; *Price:* $950; *Grade Level:* General; *Hardware:* See distributor; *Software:* See distributor; *Distributor:* EBSCO.

Provides access to virtually all English language nursing journals, publications of the American Nurses' Association, the National League for Nursing, and primary journals in more than a dozen allied health disciplines. Also includes articles from approximately 3,200 biomedical journals indexed in *Index Medicus,* 20 journals in the field of health sciences librarianship, educational, behavioral sciences, management, and popular literature. Coverage is from 1983 to the present.

Physician's Desk Reference (PDR) on CD-ROM. Producer: Medical Economics Data; *Operating System:* PC; *Subject:* Medicine; *Price:* $595; *Grade Level:* JH, HS, C; *Hardware:* IBM PC, XT, AT or compatible; 640K RAM; CD-ROM player with card, cable, monochrome or color monitor; printer (optional); *Software:* MS-DOS or PC-DOS 3.1 or higher; microsoft CD-ROM extensions; *Distributor:* EBSCO.

This is not a condensation or selection. You get the complete text of PDR for Nonprescription Drugs and PDR for Ophthalmology, and the entire contents of PDR's Drug Interactions and Side Effects Index. Contains full prescribing information on 2,800 prescriptions, over-the-counter pharmaceuticals, plus drug interactions and side effects. Features include automatic interactions checks, split screen comparisons, complete free-text word-search capabilities.

Food Analyst. Producer: Hopkins Technology; *Operating System:* PC; *Subject:* Nutrition/Reference; *Price:* $99; *Grade Level:* JH, HS, C; *Hardware:* IBM PC or compatible; 512K RAM; *Software:* PC-DOS or MS-DOS 3.1, 3.3 or higher; Microsoft CD-ROM extensions; *Distributor:* EBSCO.

A complete nutritional analysis software program that breaks down what you eat into specific nutrients such as calories, fat, sugar, protein, cholesterol, and more. The data is based on the USDA's entire, up-to-date food nutrient database, Standard Reference (Handbook 8), USDA's Home Economics Research Report 48 on sugars, and Quaker Oats food data. Direct access to over 80 nutrients/approximately 5,000 foods provided. Tracks any number of meals, recipes, and people. Very easy to use.

Food Analyst Plus. *Operating System:* PC; *Subject:* Nutrition/Reference; *Price:* $199; *Grade Level:* JH, HS, C; *Hardware:* IBM PC or compatible; 512K RAM; CD Player; printer for text; 1 floppy. Hard disk recommended; *Software:* See distributor; *Distributor:* EBSCO.

A complete nutritional analysis software program that breaks down what you eat into specific nutrients. Data is based on USDA's entire, up-to-date food nutrient database. Standard Reference (Handbook 8), USDA's Survey Data, Canadian Nutrient File 1988 (French/English), USDA's Home Economics Research Report 48 on sugars, and over 8,000 food manufacturer's brand name food products. Direct access up to 100 nutrients/approximately 22,000 foods is provided. Can export personal data files for statistical use.

Health Source CD-ROM. *Producer:* EBSCO and others; *Operating System:* PC; *Subject:* Health; *Price:* See distributor; *Grade Level:* General; *Hardware:* IBM PC, XT or compatible, 640K RAM; 5MB hard disk space available; CD-ROM player with interface card and cable; one double-sided drive; monitor; printer optional; *Software:* See distributor; *Distributor:* EBSCO.

Contains abstracts and indexing for comprehensive list of journals plus full text for selected titles. Includes 160 journals in the fields of consumer products, diet and nutrition, exercise, drugs and alcohol, and medical self-care. Searchable full text included for approximately 15 of these journals.

HISTORY

Desert Storm— The War in the Gulf. *Producer:* Warner New Media; *Operating System:* MAC; *Subject:* History; *Price:* $44.49; *Grade Level:* JH, HS; *Hardware:* Macintosh with at least 1MB of memory; *Software:* Macintosh System Software 6.0.5; *Distributor:* EBSCO.

Time correspondent files covering the war, personal profiles of Saddam Hussein and other key figures, maps of the Gulf area, a glossary of high tech weapons, and a photo gallery. A synopsis of each week's events is presented with topics covering the Battle, Economic Fallout, How CNN Phoned Home, the Home Front, a View from Exile, the European Allies, History, and Essay. Original story reports from around the world are included, as written, before they were integrated into final form by *Time* editors. Exclusive audio reports, including as-it's-happening correspondent analyses are also on the disc. The more than 400 photographs are viewable in both full color or black and white.

European Monarchs. *Operating System:* PC; *Subject:* History; *Price:* $99; *Grade Level:* General; *Hardware:* See distributor; *Software:* Included; *Distributor:* CD-ROM, Inc.

A veritable "Who's Who" of the stranger than fiction world of European kings and queens. Birth and death dates, years of succession, election, coronation, and removal, wife's and husband's name and family heritage, quotes, tales. Text search.

History of Western Civilization. *Producer:* Queue; *Operating System:* PC; *Subject:* History/Music/Literature; *Price:* $125; *Grade Level:* HS; *Hardware:* See distributor; *Software:* See distributor; *Distributor:* CDiscovery.

Supplement and review classroom instruction on Western Civilization. The titles include: History of Western Civilization—a comprehensive collection of drill and practice exercises on geography, chronology, and identifications in world history; Ancient Civilization—interactive drills based on a variety of early civilizations; European History—important events in Europe from the Middle Ages through the Age of Enlightenment; Review Questions in World History—a challenging quiz in Western Civilizations with over 400 drill and practice questions; Arts and Humanities—introduces the history of art and music plus a program on philosophy; Literature—survey of European literature from ancient to modern times.

History Source CD-ROM. *Producer:* EBSCO; *Operating System:* PC; *Subject:* History; *Price:* See distributor; *Grade Level:* General; *Hardware:* IBM PC, XT, or compatible, 640K RAM, 5MB hard disk space available; CD-ROM player with interface card and cable; one double-sided drive; VGA or super VGA monitor; *Software:* MS-DOS 3.2 or higher; Microsoft MS-DOS CD-ROM extensions version 2.1; *Distributor:* EBSCO.

Provides abstract and index coverage for 50 journals dedicated to historical research.

The First Electronic Jewish Bookshelf. *Operating System:* PC; *Subject:* Judaism, History; *Price:* $79; *Grade Level:* General; *Hardware:* See distributor; *Software:* See distributor; *Distributor:* CD-ROM, Inc.

This first electronic production of a "Jewish Bookshelf" contains thousands of interesting facts about Jews, Judaism, and Israel. Variety of data with subjects: music, humor, law, lore, history, folktales, and an encyclopedia of Judaism. Pictures and drawings.

Lessons in American History. *Producer:* Queue; *Operating System:* PC; *Subject:* History; *Price:* $135; *Grade Level:* JH, HS; *Hardware:* See distributor; *Software:* See distributor; *Distributor:* CDiscovery.

A collection of American history tutorials that are highly interactive and provide immediate feedback to ensure comprehension of the material. The titles include: Lessons in American History—detailed approach that examines trends and themes in American History; Reviewing American History I–III—chronological compulation of college board achievement test-type multiple choice questions; American History Achievement Test—review and instruction for the CEEB Achievement test that covers the pre–Colombian period to the present; SEI American History—major events and significant people in American History from the Age of Exploration through the 70s; Review Questions in American History—drill and practice covering the colonization period to the Kennedy presidency; American Presidents—extensive biographical and historical information on the lives and presidencies of our nation's leaders from Washington to Reagan.

Middle East Diary on CD-ROM. *Producer:* Quanta Press; *Operating System:* PC/MAC; *Subject:* Geography, History; *Price:* $186.50; *Grade Level:* General; *Hardware:* See distributor; *Software:* See distributor; *Distributor:* EBSCO.

The Middle East Diary on CD-ROM represents a lengthy review of Middle East history, personalities, and conflicts. This timely disc gives the end-user all the background needed to make competent decisions on travel, business, and relations in any of the volatile Middle Eastern states.

North American Indians. *Producer:* Quanta Press; *Operating System:* PC/MAC; *Subject:* Indians; *Price:* $136.50; *Grade Level:* JH, HS; *Hardware:* See distributor; *Software:* See distributor; *Distributor:* EBSCO.

A text/image database on the history of Native Americans. Included are leadership, tribal heritage, religion, family life, and customs.

The Presidents: It All Started with George. *Operating System:* PC; *Subject:* Presidents/History; *Price:* $149; *Grade Level:* Elem., JH, HS;

Hardware: See distributor; *Software:* See distributor; *Distributor:* UP-DATA.

Discover the personal and political lives, careers, campaigns, and the social and historical times of each of our presidents. Thomas Jefferson described the presidency as a "splendid misery"; Harry Truman thought it was "like riding a tiger." This interactive CD-ROM encyclopedia includes more than 1,000 full-screen color photographs in MCGA format, a presidential trivia game, narrated photo essays on the presidency and the political process, 33 video clips of significant presidential moments, a pop-up glossary, political party index, text and audio of famous speeches, social and political timeline, election facts, figures and maps, and personal glimpses of each president.

Terrorist Group Profiles. *Operating System:* PC/MAC; *Subject:* History; *Price:* $136.50; MAC $129; PC $129; *Grade Level:* JH, HS; *Hardware:* See distributor; *Software:* See distributor; *Distributor:* EBSCO.

Contains detailed biographical, statistical, and chronological information on more than 50 terrorist organizations and their membership world-wide. Group name or acronym, date formed, membership numbers, headquarters, area of operation, leadership, sponsors, objectives, targets, background, and a chronology of their operations are provided.

Time Table of History—Science and Innovation. *Operating System:* PC/MAC; *Subject:* History; *Price:* $130; *Grade Level:* K–C; *Hardware:* IBM PC/Macintosh; *Software:* See distributor; *Distributor:* CDiscovery.

Includes over 6,000 stories chronicling events that led to a high technology society. Covers computing, cryptology, television, telecommunications, time measurement, typography, weaponry, mathematics, electricity and the role of women in the advancement of science. Includes special graphics, sound, and animation.

U.S. History on CD-ROM. *Operating System:* PC/MAC; *Subject:* History; *Price:* $395; *Grade Level:* General; *Hardware:* VGA Monitor/1MB Ram; *Software:* See distributor; *Distributor:* UPDATA.

Full text of 107 books relating to U.S. History from the arrival of Native Americans to the present plus over 1,000 beautiful VGA photos, maps and tables of historical events. A sample listing includes American Home Front, America's Drug Front, Black Americans, Exploring the West, Gettysburg, American Military History, Apollo Expeditions to the Moon, Clash of Cultures, Ford's Theatre, Our Country. Eight volumes.

U.S. Presidents. *Operating System:* PC/MAC; *Subject:* History; *Price:* $99; *Grade Level:* General; *Hardware:* See distributor; *Software:* See distributor; *Distributor:* Bureau of Electronic Publishing.

Biographical and statistical information on the 41 men who have served in the highest office of the land: the date and city of the presidents' birth; their family background and ancestry; religion; first ladies and children; major events occurring in each term and much more.

USA Wars: Civil War. *Producer:* Quanta Press; *Operating System:* PC/MAC; *Subject:* History; *Price:* $136.50; *Grade Level:* JH, HS, C; *Hardware:* See distributor; *Software:* See distributor; *Distributor:* EBSCO.

The text/image/sound database encompasses the war that tore the United States apart from 1860 to 1865. Includes biographies, chronology, campaigns, battles, and foreign involvement.

USA Wars: Korea. *Producer:* Quanta Press; *Operating System:* PC/MAC; *Subject:* History; *Price:* $129; *Grade Level:* JH, HS, C; *Hardware:* Macintosh/IBM PC; *Software:* See distributor; *Distributor:* CDiscovery.

A multi-media database with 1,000 photographs of leaders, commanders, equipment, campaigns, and lines. Interviews with Korean War veterans. Major sections include biographies, glossaries, campaigns, and U.N. forces.

USA Wars: Vietnam. *Producer:* Quanta Press; *Operating System:* PC/MAC; *Subject:* History; *Price:* $129; *Grade Level:* JH, HS, C; *Hardware:* IBM/PC/MAC; *Software:* See distributor; *Distributor:* CDiscovery.

Covers the U.S. involvement in the Vietnam conflict. It includes special and general operations, order of battles, major unit histories, black-and-white and color battle images, order of military rank, medals and awards, biographies, statistics, equipment, missions, chronology, glossaries, and the entire Vietnam memorial database.

USA Wars: World War II. *Operating System:* PC/MAC; *Subject:* History; *Price:* $53.95; *Grade Level:* JH, HS; *Hardware:* IBM PC; *Software:* See distributor; *Distributor:* New Media Source.

A photographic retrospective of America's entrance into the war; participation in and fighting the war; and finally the victory over world tyranny. Contains approximately 1,000 photographs as well as descriptions. A chronology of events and biographies of some of the military and political players are included. Fourth release in series.

INDEXES

Applied Science and Technology Index. Producer: The W. H. Wilson Company; *Operating System:* PC: *Subject:* Science; *Price:* $1,495; *Grade Level:* JH, HS, C; *Hardware:* IBM Personal System/2 series of computes or any IBM PC with 640K RAM; fixed-disk drive or any WILSONLINE workstation; *Software:* PC-DOS or MS-DOS, Microsoft CD-ROM extensions; *Distributor:* EBSCO.

Provides access to timely scientific and technical information. Indexes 335 key science and technology periodical articles; includes title enhancement for articles with ambiguous title; extensive cross-referencing; complete bibliographic data; also a separate index of book reviews.

Biography Index. Producer: The W. H. Wilson Company; *Operating System:* PC; *Subject:* Reference; *Price:* $1,095; *Grade Level:* General; *Hardware:* IBM Personal System/2 series of computers or any IBM PC with 640K RAM; fixed-disk drive or any WILSONLINE Workstation; *Software:* PC-DOS or MS-DOS, Microsoft CD-ROM extensions; *Distributor:* EBSCO.

More than 2,700 periodicals of every kind. Current English language books including more than 1,800 works of individual and collective biography annually. Autobiographies, memoirs, journals, diaries, letters, interviews, bibliographies, and obituaries. Fiction, drama, pictorial works, and poetry. Juvenile literature. Biographical information from otherwise non-biographical works.

Business Periodicals Index. Producer: H. W. Wilson; *Operating System:* PC; *Subject:* Business/Reference; *Price:* $900; *Grade Level:* General; *Hardware:* See distributor; *Software:* See distributor; *Distributor:* EBSCO/H. W. Wilson.

Indexes 344 of today's leading business magazines. Business Periodicals Index features extensive cross-referencing; articles indexed under specific business headings; complete bibliographic citation; book reviews. Updated information delivered periodically.

Education Index. Producer: H. W. Wilson; *Operating System:* PC; *Subject:* Education/Reference; *Price:* $1,295; *Grade Level:* General; *Hardware:* IBM Personal System/2 series of computers or any IBM PC with 640K RAM; fixed disk or any WILSONLINE Workstation; *Software:* PC-DOS or MS-DOS, Microsoft CD-ROM extensions; *Distributor:* EBSCO.

The current information on all aspects of education. This disc offers complete indexing of 339 English language periodicals, yearbooks, and monographic series from around the world. Complete bibliographic information.

Essay and General Literature Index. *Producer:* H. W. Wilson; *Operating System:* PC; *Subject:* Literature; *Price:* $695; *Grade Level:* JH, HS, C; *Hardware:* IBM Personal System/2 series of computers or any IBM PC with 640K RAM; fixed disk drive or any WILSONLINE Workstation; *Software:* PC-DOS or MS-DOS, Microsoft CD-ROM extensions; *Distributor:* EBSCO.

This disc provides access to essays and articles in English-language essay collections and anthologies, emphasizing the humanities and social sciences.

Humanities Index. *Producer:* H. W. Wilson; *Operating System:* PC; *Subject:* Reference; *Price:* $1,295; *Grade Level:* JH, HS; *Hardware:* IBM Personal System/2 series of computers or any IBM PC with 640K RAM; fixed disk drive or any WILSONLINE Workstation; *Software:* PC-DOS or MS-DOS, Microsoft CD-ROM extensions; *Distributor:* EBSCO.

Thorough, accurate indexing of 345 English-language periodicals. Students, teachers, researchers, and librarians rely on Humanities Index for easy access to timely information in the fields of archaeology, dance, history, journalism, performing arts, religion, and other disciplines in the humanities.

Infotrac. *Producer:* Information Access; *Operating System:* PC; *Subject:* Reference; *Price:* Prices vary according to package; *Grade Level:* General; *Hardware:* IBM PC or compatible 640K RAM; *Software:* See distributor; *Distributor:* Information Access.

Indexes magazine articles. Full text, abstracts, citations available. Customer may design own package according to needs.

The Music Index on CD-ROM. *Producer:* Chadwyck-Healey; *Operating System:* PC; *Subject:* Music; *Price:* $1,250 annually; *Grade Level:* General; *Hardware:* IBM or compatible with 640K RAM and a minimum 2MB; MS-DOS 3.1 or higher and MSCDEX; *Software:* CD Answer Retrieval Software copyright 1990 by Dataware Technologies, Inc.; *Distributor:* Chadwyck-Healey, Inc.

Indexes music periodical literature duplicating data from 1981 to 1988 print volumes of *Music Index.* Boolean searches are possible.

Place-Name Index. *Producer:* Buckmaster Publishing; *Operating System:* PC; *Subject:* Reference; *Price:* $295; *Grade Level:* JH, HS, C;

Hardware: IBM PC, XT, AT, PS/2 or compatible; 640K RAM; one floppy drive; CD-ROM player with card, cable; *Software:* PC-DOS or MS-DOS 3.1 or higher, Microsoft CD-ROM extensions; *Distributor:* EBSCO. Contains place names in the United States collected from the quadrangle maps of the U.S. Geological Survey. Contains information on place names, state, county, feature type FIPS code (state/county), elevation, longitude/latitude, quadrangle map name and serial number. Each of the 1,087,000+ records contain map features such as populated places, locales, hospitals, schools, cemeteries, dams, as well as lakes, rivers, valleys, trails, parks, caves, beaches, etc.

Primary Search. *Producer:* EBSCO; *Operating System:* PC: *Subject:* Reference; *Price:* $349 (one disc); $449 (three discs); *Grade Level:* Elem., JH; *Hardware:* 640K RAM; 5MB hard disk space avail., CD-ROM player with interface card and cable; one double-sided drive, monitor, printer (optional); *Software:* MS-DOS 3.2 or higher; Microsoft MS-DOS CD-ROM extensions version 2.1; *Distributor:* EBSCO.

Primary Search is designed specifically for elementary and junior high schools. It includes eight years of abstracts and indexing for all articles from 80 magazines. It also includes full text coverage of over 3,000 Magill Book Reviews and four publications: *Newsweek, Science News, American Heritage,* and *School Library Journal.* It provides access to the magazine articles mostly used by primary students. The menu driven software is easy to use with little or no instruction. Primary Search is the perfect search tool for young researchers.

Readers' Guide to Periodical Literature. *Producer:* H. W. Wilson; *Operating System:* PC; *Subject:* Reference; *Price:* $1,095; *Grade Level:* JH, HS; *Hardware:* IBM Personal System/2 series of computers or any IBM PC with 640K RAM; fixed-disk drive or any WILSONLINE Workstation; *Software:* PC-DOS or MS-DOS, Microsoft CD-ROM extensions; *Distributor:* EBSCO.

Indexes 191 popular magazines, central to any school, college or public library collection.

LANGUAGE

A+ French. *Producer:* Queue; *Operating System:* PC/MAC; *Subject:* Language; *Price:* $195; *Grade Level:* Elem., JH, HS; *Hardware:* See distributor; *Software:* See distributor; *Distributor:* CDiscovery.

Complete French grammar source with drills in vocabulary and reading comprehension that provides students with interactivity, immediate feedback and remediation after each incorrect response. In addition there are special bonus programs in German, Latin, and Italian. These include French for Kids, Complete French Grammar I–XV, French Reading Comprehension Series, French Grammar Review I & II, Le Grand Concours. The bonus programs include the German Contest, German Grammar Review I & II, Italian Grammar Review, and Latin Grammar Review.

A + Spanish. Producer: Queue; *Operating System:* MAC; Subject: Language; *Price:* $195; *Grade Level:* Elem., JH, HS; *Hardware:* See distributor; *Software:* See distributor; *Distributor:* CDiscovery.

Complete tutorial package and interactive lessons in Spanish vocabulary, grammar, and reading comprehension that includes the following programs: Clear Spanish, the Spanish Contest, Spanish for Kids, Spanish Grammar Review I & II, Complete Spanish Grammar Package, Spanish Reading Comprehension Series, Spanish Structure Drills, and Spanish Vocabulary Drills.

The Amazing Moby. Producer: ALDE Publishing; *Operating System:* PC; *Subject:* Language; *Price:* $403; *Grade Level:* HS; *Hardware:* IBM XT, AT, 386 or compatible; 512K RAM; *Software:* PC-DOS or MS-DOS, Microsoft CD-ROM extensions; *Distributor:* EBSCO.

Over one million English words and phrases, their definitions, pronunciation, and hyphenation. It contains: a half-million single word entries and over 100,000 word phrases, which a user can use to find unwanted clichés in his or her writing; 150,000 hyphenated words, 150,000 fully pronounced words; and 200,000 words and phrases categorized by parts of speech, useable in speech syntheses applications; 9,000 stars and their coordinates are listed.

Creative Writing. Producer: Pelican and Queue; *Operating System:* PC; *Subject:* Writing; *Price:* $125; *Grade Level:* Elem., JH, HS; *Hardware:* See distributor; *Software:* See distributor; *Distributor:* CDiscovery.

Best-selling programs from Pelican Software—Pow! Zap! Kerplunk! The Comic Book Maker, Dinosaur Days, Monsters and Make Believe, Robot Writer, and the Bible Story Publisher. These programs include an easy to use word processor, colorful backgrounds, and different printout sizes. The unusual graphics encourage children to write and print out their own written and illustrated creations. Teachers and parents can use these programs to create worksheets, arts and crafts activities, bulletin board displays, and more.

Developing Writing Skills. Producer: Queue; *Operating System:* PC; *Subject:* Writing; *Price:* $295; *Grade Level:* JH, HS; *Hardware:* See distributor; *Software:* See distributor; *Distributor:* CDiscovery.

Hundreds of hours of interactive lessons helps learners improve their writing skills. A variety of question formats maintain student interest and immediate feedback encourages success. The programs include: Learning to Write, Basic English Composition Package, Developing Writing Skills, Practicing Writing Skills, Practical Composition Series, Dictionary Skills, How to Do Research, and Usage.

Playing with Language Series. Producer: Syracuse Language Systems; *Operating System:* MPC; *Subject:* Language; *Price:* $89 each (Spanish, French, English, German); *Grade Level:* Elem., JH, HS; *Hardware:* See distributor; *Software:* See distributor; *Distributor:* Bureau of Electronic Publishing.

See, Hear, Learn! Just the sight of colorful objects flashing on the screen will be enough to stimulate children of all ages, even as young as three, to play these fun games, and challenge them to learn a new language at the same time.

The discs contain games which turn learning everyday words for objects, colors, shapes, sizes, body parts, clothing, animals, fruit, vegetables, classroom objects, numbers, home objects, and telling time, into an exciting introduction to a second language. While having fun, a child using an Introducing Games disc can learn over 200 words and phrases emphasized in the first year of a typical elementary school second language program. Not only are children more eager to learn, but they also pick up languages more quickly, especially with the use of the interactive games and stories. Many of the games were designed to have equivalent "real-life" versions such as Simon Says, the Jigsaw Puzzles, and Bingo, which can be played with parents or used by teachers in a classroom setting.

Each Introductory Games disc contains 27 games with high resolution graphics and audio. The game to be played is easily chosen from a friendly pictorial menu, and most games are proceeded by a practice screen that introduces new vocabulary items. Starting with simple object and color identification, the progressive levels include sequential and spatial memory games, learning everyday words like the parts of the face, and various clothing names, prepositions, verbs, and possessives.

All communication by the computer to the user during the games are in the new language; there are no instructions in English or translations, which also helps to increase learning.

Crossword Cracker. *Operating System:* PC; *Subject:* Language; *Price:* $59; *Grade Level:* JH, HS; *Hardware:* See distributor; *Software:* See distributor; *Distributor:* Bureau of Electronic Publishing.

To figure out a crossword answer in seconds, just type in the letters you know and the length of the word, and Crossword Cracker will supply the word—works as a great spell checker too! Anagram answers are even easier; by supplying the list of letters in the word, Margana supplies all the nearest matches.

Learn to Speak Series. *Producer:* Educorp; *Operating System:* PC/MPC/MAC; *Subject:* Language; *Price:* $79 each; Offered also in Learn to Speak Spanish—MPC; Learn to Speak Spanish—MAC; Learn to Speak French—MPC; Learn to Speak French—MAC; Lingua—ROM II—MAC; Learn to Speak English (Spanish)—MAC; Learn to Speak English (French)—MAC; Learn to Speak English (English)—MAC; Learn to Speak English (Japanese)—MAC; *Grade Level:* JH, HS; *Hardware:* MPC PC; *Software:* HyperCard 2.0; *Distributor:* UPDATA.

Language courses which emphasize speaking and listening comprehension skills. Between 30 to 36 lessons depending on the individual language. Native speakers read dialogues based on real-life situations such as arriving in the country where the language is spoken, getting settled, dealing with emergencies, going out socially, buying things, and going to the doctor. Listening exercises help you master understanding of the spoken language, while interactive drills help you master the grammar. These drills can be modified by you to accommodate many correct ways of expressing the same thought and you are re-drilled on missed answers. There are cultural notes and grammar reference materials available for your use. You can record your own voice for comparison to the speaker's voice.

Mastering English Grammar. *Producer:* Queue; *Operating System:* MAC; *Subject:* English; *Price:* $395; *Grade Level:* Elem., JH, HS, C; *Hardware:* See distributor; *Software:* See distributor; *Distributor:* CDiscovery.

Comprehensive collection of 47 best-selling grammar programs including the entire Practical Grammar Series I, II, III, working with sentences and learning parts of speech.

LINGUAROM II. *Operating System:* MPC/MAC; *Subject:* Foreign Language; *Price:* $589; *Grade Level:* Elem., JH, HS; *Hardware:* See distributor; *Software:* See distributor; *Distributor:* Bureau of Electronic Publishing.

For the most diverse language tutor try this collection of 30 HyperGlot language programs to learn Spanish, French, German, Russian, Italian, Chinese, and Japanese. Each language tutor includes introductory lessons as well as noun, verb, and grammar tutors. They also include "wordtortures" which give a rigorous drill on 1400 to 1600 of the most commonly used verbs, nouns, adjectives, adverbs, and comparatives to show what you've learned (or haven't learned)! This drill feature also includes a retest for the words you miss.

Littérature Française. Operating System: PC; *Subject:* French literature; *Price:* $495; *Grade Level:* JH, HS; *Hardware:* See distributor; *Software:* See distributor; *Distributor:* Bureau of Electronic Publishing.

This extraordinary abstract of French literature is perfect for any French-speaking literature addict. The volume includes a chronology of events from A.D. 888 through A.D. 1899.

Voilà! Producer: Queue; *Operating System:* MAC; *Subject:* French; *Price:* $295; *Grade Level:* Elem., JH, HS, C; *Hardware:* See distributor; *Software:* See distributor; *Distributor:* CDiscovery.

Interactive French language tutor that develops and reinforces linguistic skills by providing a sampling of French literature and song for students from early-intermediate through advanced levels. The program includes Fables de la Fontaine, Coquerico!, Selections Françaises, Les Petits Chanteurs de Paris, Chansons Françaises pour les Enfants, Contes de Charles Perrault, La Vie de Jean-Philippe, Chansons de la Vieille France, Echos de France: Paris, and Echos de France: Les Provinces.

Languages of the World. Producer: NTC Publishing Group; *Operating System:* PC; *Subject:* Language/Reference; *Price:* $950; *Grade Level:* JH, HS; *Hardware:* IBM PC, AT or compatible and CD-ROM drive; *Software:* Microsoft extensions; *Distributor:* EBSCO.

Multilingual dictionary database containing 18 multilingual or bilingual dictionaries which enable users to translate words or phrases among 12 different languages. Together with its dictionary search system this CD-ROM can also be used with the most commonly used word-processing systems. Complete dictionary entries can be searched as well as instantaneous translations.

Ole! Producer: Queue; *Operating System:* MAC; *Subject:* Spanish; *Price:* $295; *Grade Level:* Elem., JH, HS; *Hardware:* See distributor; *Software:* See distributor; *Distributor:* CDiscovery.

Interactive Spanish tutor that involves learners through Spanish and Latin American songs, folk tales, poetry, prose and drama. Includes Los Melindres de Belisa, a Treasury of Spanish Folk Songs, Spanish Songs for Children, Golden Treasury of Spanish American Verse, and many more.

Poem Finder. *Operating System:* PC; *Subject:* Literature; *Price:* $300; *Grade Level:* JH, HS, C; *Hardware:* See distributor; *Software:* See distributor; *Distributor:* CD-ROM, Inc.

Poem Finder is the largest, most comprehensive, and most current poetry index. It has over 270,000 poems, from antiquity to today. The poetry has over 1,300 anthologies and over 1,300 single-author collections, and 100 periodicals. Keyword searching through all fields. Boolean searching using up to four operators (and, or, not, between).

Reading Horizons and Mastery Drill and Practice. *Operating System:* PC; *Subject:* Reading; *Price:* $2,590; *Grade Level:* JH, HS; *Hardware:* See distributor; *Software:* See distributor; *Distributor:* UPDATA.

This low level reading and spelling courseware guides the student (English speaking or English as a second language) through the 42 sounds of the alphabet, five phonetic, and two decoding skills. In total, there are 30 lessons each with its own human voice soundtrack. Reading instruction given on CD-ROM is more individualized because of the branching and random access capabilities that help students review and practice concepts they may not have understood. The courseware includes a management system with reports, interactive testing and record keeping with pre, post, and four interim tests. No prior reading or keyboarding skills are required to use the program which is designed for the interdependent use, even for non-readers, and it can effectively teach individuals, small groups or entire classes. Also available on this disc is the Mastery Drill and Practice with 1,500 vocabulary words in groups which correspond to the phonics lesson that they may have just completed in Reading Horizons. Definitions context and reading practice are available for each word with graphic representations, voice comparison, and decoding practice.

Reasoning Skills. *Producer:* Queue; *Operating System:* PC; *Subject:* Reading and Thinking; *Price:* $95; *Grade Level:* Elem., JH, HS; *Hardware:* See distributor; *Software:* See distributor; *Distributor:* CDiscovery.

Contains over 20 programs for reading comprehension, logic, and critical thinking. The titles include reading and thinking, reading and critical thinking, lessons in logic and reading reasoning.

LITERATURE

CD CoreWorks. Producer: Roth Publishing, Inc.; *Operating System:* PC; *Subject:* Poetry, drama, literature; *Price:* $475; *Grade Level:* JH, HS; *Hardware:* IBM XT, 286, 386 or fully compatible computer; hard disk with 1.2MB; 640K RAM; *Software:* PC/MS-DOS 3.0; CD-ROM Drive using Microsoft extensions 1.1 or higher; *Distributor:* EBSCO.

Access poetry, essays, drama, and short stories in a single integrated index database and search program. CD CoreWorks contains over a half million searchable data fields that can be retrieved quickly and easily.

Classic Collection. Producer: CMC ReSearch, Inc.; *Operating System:* MAC; *Subject:* Literature; *Price:* $79; *Grade Level:* HS, C; *Hardware:* See distributor; *Software:* See distributor; *Distributor:* CD-ROM, Inc.

A three-disc set containing Shakespeare, Sherlock Holmes, and Birds of America Multimedia.

Classic Collection Plus. Operating System: MAC; *Subject:* Literature; *Price:* $99; *Grade Level:* HS, C; *Hardware:* See distributor; *Software:* See distributor; *Distributor:* CD-ROM, Inc.

A four-disc set containing Multimedia Birds of America, Multimedia Audubon's Mammals, Shakespeare, and Sherlock Holmes.

DisLit. Producer: OCLC/G.K. Hall; *Operating System:* PC; *Subject:* Literature; *Price:* $995; *Grade Level:* HS, C; *Hardware:* PC compatible or PS/2 microcomputer with 640K RAM and 20MB hard drive plus a CD-ROM drive with MS-DOS extensions 2.0 or higher; *Software:* See distributor for required search software; *Distributor:* OCLC.

Primary value lies in searches on 143 authors from selected TUSAS. Many volumes were published in the 1960s and 1970s. Can be very useful for serious high school researchers as well as college undergraduates.

Electronic Home Library. Producer: World Library, Inc.; *Operating System:* PC; *Subject:* Literature; *Price:* $295; *Grade Level:* HS; *Hardware:* IBM PC, XT, AT, 386, or compatible hard disk, 640K RAM; CD-ROM player; *Software:* MS-DOS or PC-DOS, Microsoft extensions; *Distributor:* EBSCO.

This disc includes the complete text of 250 selected works from the *Library of the Future,* 1st edition. Just imagine Aristotle, Plato, Melville, Conan Doyle, Tolstoy, Dana, Kant, and many more, all at your fingertips, all on one disc.

Great Literature. *Operating System:* PC/MAC; *Subject:* Literature; *Price:* $99; *Grade Level:* HS, C; *Hardware:* See distributor; *Software:* See distributor; *Distributor:* Bureau of Electronic Publishing.

Great Literature Classic Edition is the ultimate literature collection. Starting where many other book and CD-ROM collections end, Great Literature includes pictures, full color illustrations, engravings, and spoken passages which truly enhance the power of the written word. You'll hear narrations of these classics by George Kennedy, Bob Saget, and others. Imagine hearing Romeo's speech to Juliet accompanied with color illustrations of Romeo and Juliet, or hearing Poe's "The Raven" accompanied with black and white illustrations. Great Literature includes over 360 great works ranging from the 20th century back to ancient history—all compiled from classic authoritative editions. A simple user interface makes it easy to read, browse through this vast collection of books, and instantly search by word, event, book, picture, or article. This disc is a fantastic resource for libraries, schools, historians, students, and anyone else who enjoys the great works of literature. It's the ultimate multimedia library.

Greatest Books Ever Written. *Producer:* World Library; *Operating System:* PC; *Subject:* Literature; *Price:* $295; *Grade Level:* JH, HS; *Hardware:* See distributor; *Software:* See distributor; *Distributor:* UP-DATA.

Many of the most highly regarded books of Western literature are included on this disc along with engravings, pictures, and audio excerpts. Authors and titles include Lewis Carroll, A. Conan Doyle (*Adventures of Sherlock Holmes*), Tolstoy (*Anna Karenina, War and Peace*), *Wuthering Heights, The Autobiography of Benjamin Franklin,* Dostoyevsky (*Brothers Karamazov*), Voltaire (*Candide*), Chaucer (*Canterbury Tales*), Dickens (*David Copperfield, Great Expectations, A Tale of Two Cities*), Darwin (*Descent of Man*), Emerson (*Essays*), Homer (*Iliad, Odyssey*), G. B. Shaw, Plato (*Republic*), Jack London, Daniel Defoe, Nathaniel Hawthorne, Jules Verne, Thoreau, Twain, and more.

Masterplots II CD-ROM. *Producer:* Salem Press; *Operating System:* PC; *Subject:* Literature; *Price:* $399; *Grade Level:* JH, HS, C; *Hardware:* PC, XT, or compatible computer; 640K RAM; CD-ROM player with interface card and cable; one double-sided drive; monitor; printer (optional); *Software:* MS-DOS 3.2 or higher; Microsoft MS-DOS CD-ROM extensions version 2.1; *Distributor:* EBSCO.

Masterplots II provides discussions of plot, which clearly convey the action of the work while focusing on the work's theme, style and characters, for more than 2,500 works of literature. Searchers can find works by a particular author, with a similar theme, set in a specific country or point in history, or by title, character name or date of publication. Corresponds to the printed volumes *Masterplots II, American Fiction Series* (1986); *Masterplots II, Short Story Series* (1986); *Masterplots II, British and Commonwealth Fiction Series* (1987); *Masterplots II, World Fiction Series* (1988); *Masterplots II, Nonfiction Series* (1989); *Masterplots II, Drama Series* (1990); *Masterplots II, Juvenile and Young Adult Fiction Series* (1991); *Cyclopedia of World Authors II* (1989); and *Cyclopedia of Literary Characters II* (1990). Updates applicable since publication of print volumes will be included on the CD-ROM.

Shakespeare on Disc. *Producer:* CMC ReSearch; *Operating System:* PC; *Subject:* Literature; *Price:* $104; *Grade Level:* HS, C; *Hardware:* See distributor; *Software:* See distributor; *Distributor:* EBSCO.

Complete unabridged works of Shakespeare. Includes both Queen's English and modern versions.

Sherlock Holmes on Disc. *Producer:* CMC ReSearch, Inc.; *Operating System:* PC/MAC; *Subject:* Sherlock Homes Stories; *Price:* $59; *Grade Level:* General; *Hardware:* See distributor; *Software:* See distributor; *Distributor:* CDiscovery.

Contains full text of all Sir Arthur Conan Doyle's Sherlock Holmes stories plus original *Strand Magazine* illustrations by Baget. Linoleum block prints by Dr. George Wells accent the Holmes stories. Dr. George S. Bascom (poet laureate for the Harvard Medical School class of 1952) has written intriguing and beautiful medical poetry included on the disc. Full word search, browsing, and traditional table of contents are available.

Wordcruncher Disc. *Operating System:* PC; *Subject:* Literature; *Price:* $239; *Grade Level:* General; *Hardware:* See distributor; *Software:* See distributor; *Distributor:* Bureau of Electronic Publishing.

Includes the *Riverside Shakespeare* and Library of America Editions and many of the works of Emerson, Cather, Franklin, Jefferson, Melville, Thoreau, Twain, Faulkner, Hawthorne, James, Whitman, and London. Also includes two Bible versions and the Constitution papers.

Library of the Future Series (First Edition). *Producer:* World Library, Inc.; *Operating System:* PC; *Subject:* Reference/Literature; *Price:* $515; *Grade Level:* JH, HS; *Hardware:* IBM PC, XT, AT, 386, or compatible;

hard disk; 640K RAM CD-ROM player; *Software:* MS-DOS or PC-DOS, Microsoft extensions; *Distributor:* EBSCO.

Gives the user instant access to 450 of the world's most important titles. Word for word reproductions of the philosophical musings of Aristotle, Kant, Confucius, and Plato. The literary and dramatic works of Chaucer, Poe, Shakespeare, Aristophanes, and others. The Magna Carta, the Constitution and a host of other important historical, political, religious, and scientific documents.

Library of the Future Series, Second Edition. All other information is the same as for the First Edition.

Gives the user instant access to 900 of the world's most important titles. The disc includes all first edition works plus an additional 500 titles, all on one CD. Authors include Aesop, Plutarch, Thoreau, and many more. Androcles and the Lion, Aemilius Pauls, and a host of other important historical, political, religious, and scientific documents — including every phrase, every word, every punctuation mark.

MATH

Mastering Math. *Producer:* Queue; *Operating System:* MAC/PC; *Subject:* Math; *Price:* $195; *Grade Level:* Elem., JH; *Hardware:* See distributor; *Software:* See distributor; *Distributor:* CDiscovery.

Interactive drill and instruction with immediate feedback assists students in learning math. The programs in this math series include math word problems, sports problems, fraction word problems, special topics in math, mathematical grade 6, survival math series, and algebra word problems.

Mathsci Disc Set. *Producer:* SilverPlatter Information; *Operating System:* PC; *Subject:* Math; *Price:* $4,324; *Grade Level:* General; *Hardware:* IBM PC or compatible; 640K RAM; CD-ROM player; monitor; printer of text; one floppy drive; hard disk recommended; *Software:* PC-DOS or MS-DOS 2.1 or higher; *Distributor:* EBSCO.

The CD-ROM version of the American Mathematical Society's database with coverage for 1983 to the present. It comprises the Mathematical Reviews and more than 70,000 citations from Current Mathematical Publication. Covers the literature of mathematics and related fields such as statistics, computer science, and engineering. Individual records can be downloaded, and text software can be used to format printed documents with mathematical symbols.

MUSIC

Audio Notes. *Producer:* Warner; *Operating System:* MAC; *Subject:* Music; *Price:* $66 each; *Grade Level:* HS; *Hardware:* At least 1 Meg of RAM and hard disk drive with 6.5 MB of free space; *Software:* See distributor; *Distributor:* CDiscovery.

A new CD collection combining digital musical performances with text, pictures, and audio in an environment rich presentation controlled by the listener. Conducted by Robert Shaw, "A German Requiem" is performed in this two-disc set (including Hypercard 2.0) and enhanced by pictures, commentaries, additional music, analysis, historical information, musical glossary and index, all interactively accessible by a MAC. Features include the Harmonic Plan to explore how Brahms used harmony, instant access to any part of the music, including all the themes and their transformations. Fifty side journeys enhance the musical experience with richly illustrated biographical, historical, and musical insights.

Beethoven Symphony No. 9 CD Companion. *Producer:* Voyager; *Operating System:* PC/MAC ; *Subject:* Music; *Price:* $78; *Grade Level:* HS, C; *Hardware:* Macintosh Plus, IBM 286, MS-DOS or MS-DOS 3.1; *Software:* Hypercard; *Distributor:* UPDATA.

An interactive compact disc that combines entertainment and education. The user can listen to Beethoven's magnificent "Choral" Symphony in whole or in part while choosing from a plethora of options. The user can choose moment by moment what he wants to do: Listen while reading time-matched commentary by UCLA music professor Robert Winter, listen while viewing comments about the language of music or the life and times of Ludwig van Beethoven and more. During the vocal section of the Ninth Symphony's mighty finale, you can follow on screen the text of Schiller's "Ode to Joy," switching back and forth from English to German if you wish. You can play music passages that illustrate a particular concept, highlight words and press "Glossary," or play musical games. This can all be done while listening to the Ninth being performed by Hans Schmidt-Isserstedt conducting the Vienna State Opera and the Vienna Philharmonic.

CD Audio Stack. *Producer:* Voyager; *Operating System:* MAC; *Subject:* Music; *Price:* $99.95; *Grade Level:* JH, HS: *Hardware:* See distributor; *Software:* See distributor; *Distributor:* CDiscovery.

Audio CD's are controlled from Hypercard with this utility that allows you to play music, sounds, or spoken words including Audio Event Maker, Audio Ideas, and an on-line manual.

CD 7. Producer: Quantum Leap Technology; *Operating System:* MAC; *Subject:* Entertainment; *Price:* $99; *Grade Level:* JH, HS; *Hardware:* Any Macintosh; *Software:* See distributor; *Distributor:* EBSCO.

Large collection of Macintosh software including over 14,000 files—2,570 art, 931 games, 838 HyperCard stacks, 1,262 demo files, 1,180 digitized sounds, 1,453 music files, and over 1,000 Macintosh utilities.

Composer Quest. Operating System: MPC; *Subject:* Music/History; *Price:* $74.95; *Grade Level:* General; *Hardware:* See distributor; *Software:* See distributor; *Distributor:* New Media Source.

Interactive multimedia package which contains CD-quality recordings of great musical performances. History of music from seventeenth through twentieth centuries. Games provide additional entertainment.

A German Requiem. Producer: Warner New Media; *Operating System:* MAC; *Subject:* Music/Brahms; *Price:* $70.50; *Grade Level:* JH, HS, C; *Hardware:* 1MB RAM, hard disk drive/5–7MB free MAC compatible CD-ROM drive; *Software:* MAC system software 6.0.5 or higher; *Distributor:* EBSCO.

Greatest choral work of the Romantic era, Johannes Brahms' "A German Requiem" is performed brilliantly in this two-disc set, with Robert Shaw conducting the Atlanta Symphony Orchestra and Chorus. Pictures, commentaries, additional music, analysis, historical information, musical glossary, and index are all interactively accessible with a Macintosh computer. Use the Requiem Map to get instant access to any part of the music—including all the themes and their transformations; take more than 50 side journeys to enhance your musical experience with richly illustrated biographical, historical, and musical highlights; enhance your understanding of music with more than 500 examples of sound and music from Gregorian Chant to Britten's War Requiem; try the Harmonic Plan and explore how Brahms used harmony.

The Magic Flute. Operating System: MAC; *Subject:* Music; *Price:* $66; *Grade Level:* General; *Hardware:* See distributor; *Software:* See distributor; *Distributor:* Bureau of Electronic Publishing.

Mozart's opera "The Magic Flute," conducted by Mikolaus Haroncourt, lets you see, hear and control a complete music program. "The Magic Flute" is playable on a CD player and contains the complete opera, on-screen commentary and annotation about the opera, and extra audio tracks to expand your understanding of the opera. It also contains a broad range of visual and audio information.

Mozart "Dissonant" String Quartet in C Major. Operating System:
MAC; *Subject:* Music; *Price:* $59.95; *Grade Level:* General; *Hardware:*
See distributor; *Software:* See distributor; *Distributor:* UPDATA.
Music commentary accompanies a digital audio recording of
Mozart's String Quartet in C Major K. 465, the "Dissonant," performed
exclusively for this CD-ROM by the Angeles Quartet.

Multimedia Beethoven: The Ninth Symphony. *Operating System:* MPC;
Subject: Music; *Price:* $79; *Grade Level:* JH, HS; *Hardware:* See
distributor; *Software:* See distributor; *Distributor:* Bureau of Electronic
Publishing.
Multimedia Beethoven: The Ninth Symphony is an incredible
musical journey that will arouse your senses, stir your imagination, and
forever change the way you experience music. In five sections, you'll see
and hear everything from an overview of the symphonic form to an in-
depth analysis of each movement of the Ninth. Each section is authored
by noted UCLA music professor Robert Winter. You can even take an
interactive quiz to test the growth of your musical knowledge.

Music Box. *Operating System:* PC; *Subject:* Music; *Price:* $49; *Grade
Level:* JH, HS; *Hardware:* See distributor; *Software:* See distributor;
Distributor: Bureau of Electronic Publishing.
Music Box, a floppy diskette–based program from Trantor, brings
intuitive, graphical control of audio CD discs to any CD-ROM installa-
tion which uses the Microsoft CD-ROM extensions. The latest version in-
cludes the command line, memory-resident and Windows versions of
Music Box.

Orchestra. *Operating System:* MAC; *Subject:* Music; *Price:* $79; *Grade
Level:* JH, HS; *Hardware:* See distributor; *Software:* See distributor;
Distributor: Bureau of Electronic Publishing.
Orchestra on CD-ROM includes the full digital London recording of
"The Young Person's Guide to the Orchestra" by the London Symphony
Orchestra, conducted by Benjamin Britten. This Audio Notes program
invites you to see what instruments look like, hear how they sound and
learn how they're played. Graphics highlight who's playing them, while
a full-length, illustrated analysis explains how Britten put the piece
together.

Rite of Spring. *Operating System:* MAC; *Subject:* Music; *Price:* $79;
Grade Level: General; *Hardware:* See distributor; *Software:* See distributor; *Distributor:* Bureau of Electronic Publishing.

Contains a digital recording of Igor Stravinsky's "The Rite of Spring" featuring Charles Dutoit conducting the Orchestre Symphonique de Montreal, generous supplemental excerpts by Robert Winter and others.

Schubert: "The Trout" Quintet. Operating System: MAC; *Subject:* Music; *Price:* $59; *Grade Level:* General; *Hardware:* See distributor; *Software:* See distributor; *Distributor:* CD-ROM, Inc.

Enjoy this light-hearted, yet information-packed examination of this work of music. Included is the song—in English and the original German—on which Schubert based the quintet.

World View. Operating System: PC/MPC/MAC; *Subject:* Photography, Music; *Price:* $29.95; *Grade Level:* General; *Hardware:* See distributor; *Software:* See distributor; *Distributor:* New Media Sources.

World View contains 100 photographs of the world from above including planets and space exploration from the best of NASA's archives. One hundred soundtracks of new age piano music composed by Jamie Brehm and Kevin Mannis combine with the photographs to make an exhilarating presentation.

REFERENCE

Academic Abstracts (AA) Full Text Elite—Academic. Producer: EBSCO Publishing; *Operating System:* PC; *Subject:* Reference; *Price:* $4,499; *Grade Level:* JH, HS, C; *Hardware:* IBM PC, XT compatible 640K RAM; one double-sided drive; 5MB hard disk space available; *Software:* PC-DOS or MS-DOS 3.2 or higher; Microsoft CD-ROM extensions version 2.10; *Distributor:* EBSCO.

Academic Abstracts (AA) Full Text Elite combines key word access to abstracts or articles from 747 general interest magazines plus *The New York Times,* with key word access to full text magazine articles. Full text for 30 reference magazines, including *Newsweek, The Economist,* and *Congressional Quarterly,* is included. Also includes thousands of Magill Book Reviews by Salem Press in full text.

Book Review Digest. Producer: H. W. Wilson; *Operating System:* PC; *Subject:* Reading; *Price:* $1,095; *Grade Level:* JH, HS, C; *Hardware:* IBM Personal System/2 series of computers or any IBM PC with 640K RAM; fixed disk drive or any WILSONLINE Workstation; *Software:* PC-DOS or MS-DOS, Microsoft CD-ROM extensions; *Distributor:* EBSCO.

Provides excerpts from and citations to reviews of current and adult fiction and nonfiction from *Book Review Digest.* Covers nearly 6,000 English-language books each year.

Book of Lists #3. *Operating System:* PC/MAC; *Subject:* Reference; *Price:* $69.95; *Grade Level:* General; *Hardware:* See distributor; *Software:* See distributor; *Distributor:* New Media Source.

Trivia disc contains facts and information on a host of subjects including sports, sciences, space, entertainment, and more. Author David Wallechinsky makes sure learning through entertainment is fun.

Books in Print with Book Reviews Plus/Europe. *Producer:* R. R. Bowker Electronic Publishing; *Operating System:* PC; *Subject:* Reading/Book Reviews; *Price:* See distributor; *Grade Level:* JH, HS, C; *Hardware:* IBM PC or compatible; 512K RAM (640K recommended); CD-ROM player; two floppy disk drives (hard disk recommended) and printer; *Software:* PC-DOS or MS-DOS 3.1 or higher, Microsoft CD-ROM extension; *Distributor:* EBSCO.

Citations to over one million books currently in print from about 22,000 publishers and full text of over 80,000 book reviews. The citations correspond to those published in *Books in Print.* Subject classification scheme uses over 65,000 Library of Congress subject headings.

Books Out of Print Plus/Europe. *Producer:* R. R. Bowker Electronic Publishing; *Operating System:* PC; *Subject:* Reading/Book Reviews; *Price:* See distributor; *Grade Level:* JH, HS, C; *Hardware:* IBM PC or compatible; 512K RAM (640K recommended); CD-ROM player; two floppy drives (hard disk recommended); and printer; *Software:* PC-DOS or MS-DOS 3.0 or higher; Microsoft CD-ROM extensions; *Distributor:* EBSCO.

Citations to over 500,000 books declared to be out of print or out of stock (July 1979 to date) from roughly 22,000 publishers. Subject classification scheme uses over 65,000 Library of Congress subject headings. Corresponds to *Books Out of Print* and partly to *Books in Print* online database.

Bookshelf/Microsoft. *Producer:* Microsoft Corporation; *Operating System:* PC; *Subject:* Reference; *Price:* $295; *Grade Level:* JH, HS, C; *Hardware:* IBM PC, XT, AT, or compatible 640K RAM; CD-ROM player; monitor; printer (optional); *Software:* PC-DOS or MS-DOS 3.1 or higher, Microsoft CD-ROM extensions; *Distributor:* EBSCO.

The CD-ROM reference library and word processing tool includes complete versions of the *American Heritage Dictionary, Rogets II, Electronic Thesaurus, The 1987 World Almanac* and *Book of Facts,*

Bartlett's Familiar Quotations, The Chicago Manual of Style, Houghton Mifflin Usage Alert, U.S. Zip Code Directory, Forms and Letters, Business Information Sources, Houghton Mifflin Speller. Bookshelf works within the word processor as you are writing and is fully compatible with many popular word processor programs.

Britannica Family Choice. *Producer:* Britannica; *Operating System:* PC; *Subject:* Education, Math, Geography, Reading, Science, Grammar, etc.; *Price:* $199; *Grade Level:* Elem., JH, HS; *Hardware:* See distributor; *Software:* See distributor; *Distributor:* UPDATA.

Contains 15 educational software programs for children: Algebra I First Semester and Algebra II Second Semester, the Berenstain Bears Junior Jigsaw (10 puzzles), the Berenstain Bears Learn About Counting (basic math concepts), Body Transparent (movable bones of human body), Designasaurus (award winner for Best Educational Program 1988), Grammar Examiner (gain grammar skills while editing a newspaper), Jigsaw! The Ultimate Electronic Puzzle (for the whole family), Just Fax (creates fax cover sheets for business or home office use), Math Maze, Millionaire II (gain stock market insight), Revolution '76 (economic and military strategy), States and Traits (lakes, mountains, etc.), Super Spellicopter (spelling game), Fiction Advisor (provides list of recommended books and authors based on areas of study or interest).

Census Data. *Operating System:* PC; *Subject:* Census; *Price:* $995; *Grade Level:* JH, HS; *Hardware:* See distributor; *Software:* See distributor; *Distributor:* Bureau of Electronic Publishing.

Contains 100+ key variables from the 1990 Census by census tract, zip code, place, county, and state for the United States. Data includes key areas such as population by race, sex, age, origin.

College Boards Queue. *Producer:* College Board; *Operating System:* MAC; *Subject:* Study skills; *Price:* $195; *Grade Level:* HS, C; *Hardware:* See distributor; *Software:* See distributor; *Distributor:* CDiscovery.

Complete package to prepare students for the English SAT and ACT tests, plus the English, history, and biology Achievement Tests.

Consu/Stats I. *Producer:* Hopkins Technology; *Operating System:* PC; *Subject:* Reference; *Price:* $65; *Grade Level:* JH, HS, C; *Hardware:* IBM PC or compatible; 512K RAM; CD-ROM Drive; *Software:* PC-DOS or MS-DOS 3.1, 3.3 or higher, Microsoft CD-ROM extensions; *Distributor:* EBSCO.

The complete public use source data files on 1984 surveys of Consumer Expenditures (U.S. Census/BLS), including detailed interview and diary data. Covers hundreds of characteristics of thousands of consumer units and family members in 100 geographical areas, including income and expenditures by commodity. Also includes major appliance purchases and inventories, trips and vacations, and vehicle purchases and disposals. Over 54 million data fields in this database.

Consumer Reports on CD-ROM, 1985-Present. *Producer:* National Information Services Corporation; *Operating System:* PC; *Subject:* Reference; *Price:* $461; *Grade Level:* General; *Hardware:* IBM PC, XT, AT, PS/2 or compatible; 512K RAM; any CD-ROM drive; monochrome or color monitor; *Software:* PC-DOS or MS-DOS, Microsoft CD-ROM extensions; *Distributor:* EBSCO.

Contains the complete text of the 11 regular monthly issues of the printed *Consumer Reports*.

Consumers Reference Disc. *Producer:* National Information Services Corporation; *Operating System:* PC; *Subject:* Reference; *Price:* $811; *Grade Level:* General; *Hardware:* IBM PC, XT, AT, PS/2 or compatible; 512K RAM; any CD-ROM drive; monochrome or color monitor; *Software:* PC-DOS or MS-DOS, Microsoft CD-ROM player; *Distributor:* EBSCO.

All volumes (since 1985) of both *Consumer Index* and *Consumer Health and Nutrition Index* are included together on one disc. *Consumer Index* abstracts over 25,000 product evaluations, recalls, alerts, and warnings as well as 8,000 leading articles on travel and transportation, finances, jobs, computers, food, health, and other subjects. Consumer Reference Disc indexes over 6,000 articles each year under 4,000 medical and other subject headings from more than 80 consumer magazines, publications, and newsletters.

County-City Plus. *Operating System:* PC; *Subject:* Reference; *Price:* $199; *Grade Level:* General; *Hardware:* See distributor; *Software:* See distributor; *Distributor:* Bureau of Electronic Publishing.

An annual update and extension of the data in the Census Bureau's popular *County and City Databook* containing county summaries (data for every county and state), city statistics and data for places.

Drugs and Crime CD-ROM Library. *Producer:* Abt Books; *Operating System:* PC; *Subject:* Drugs/Crime — Social Studies; *Price:* $200; *Grade Level:* JH, HS, C; *Hardware:* IBM PC or compatible; 640K RAM; 10MB hard disk; and CD-ROM player; *Software:* PC-DOS or MS-DOS, Microsoft CD-ROM extensions; *Distributor:* EBSCO.

Abstracts, full text books, journal articles, images, and data sets from the Department of Justice. State Health and Human Services, Education, Transportation, Treasury and Defense, as well as foreign governments, the UN and private sector sources. It is an essential resource for law enforcement and other criminal justice officials as well as librarians.

Econ/Stats I. *Producer:* Hopkins Technology; *Operating System:* PC; *Subject:* Reference/Economics; *Price:* $65; *Grade Level:* HS, C; *Hardware:* IBM PC or compatible; 512K RAM; CD-ROM player; *Software:* PC-DOS or MS-DOS version 3.1, 3.3 or higher, Microsoft CD-ROM extensions; *Distributor:* EBSCO.

Contains Consumer Price Index (320 commodities and services, 50 area definitions), Producer Price Index (over 6,700 commodities), Export-Import Price Index (over 3,000 products and services), Industrial Production Index (272 commodities), Money Stock, Selected Interest Rates (90 Rates), Industry Employment Hours and Earnings by State and Areas (527 industries, 374 area definitions nearly a half-million records), and Capacity Utilization (38 industrial categories). Some data goes back to 1913.

Education Library. *Producer:* SilverPlatter; *Operating System:* PC/MAC; *Subject:* Reference; *Price:* $450 annual; *Grade Level:* General; *Hardware:* See distributor; *Software:* See distributor; *Distributor:* UP-DATA.

An international bibliography of educational materials, containing approximately 500,000 records on all types of materials, including books, journals, theses, data files, slides, newspapers, recordings, filmstrips, microforms, and manuscripts.

Gale Research Inc.: *Author Biographies and Literature Criticism CD-ROM.* *Producer:* Gale; *Operating System:* PC/MAC; *Subject:* Reference/Literature; *Price:* $500; *Grade Level:* HS, C; *Hardware:* Compatible with all major CD-ROM; *Software:* None; *Distributor:* Gale Research, Inc.

Full-text biographical essays on 300 authors, critical essays on their writings, a bibliography of their works, a list of other sources of information on the author, and a summary of media adaptations of their works. In other words, everything you need to know about an author. An update is planned every three years.

Guinness Disc of Records '90. *Producer:* UniDisc; *Operating System:* PC/MAC; *Subject:* Reference; *Price:* $149; *Grade Level:* Elem., JH, HS; *Hardware:* See distributor; *Software:* See distributor; *Distributor:* EBSCO.

Based on the all-time best selling *Guinness Book of Records* this new multimedia compact disc brings to life man and the world in which he lives. Often fascinating, the disc is always informative and yet fun to use. Records contained on the disc prove a source of authenticated facts covering everything from the scientific world to sports, games, and pastimes. The disc includes animations, music and sound effects, plus 300 full color photographs.

Guinness Multimedia of Records. *Operating System:* MAC/PC; *Subject:* Reference; *Price:* $199; *Grade Level:* General; *Hardware:* See distributor; *Software:* See distributor; *Distributor:* CDiscovery.

Locate over 6,000 world records on every topic from sports to business to natural events. Records provide a source of authenticated facts covering everything from the scientific world, to sports, games, and pastimes. Color photographs and sounds are included.

KGB World Factbook. *Operating System:* MAC; *Subject:* Reference/History; *Price:* $84; *Grade Level:* General; *Hardware:* See distributor; *Software:* See distributor; *Distributor:* CD-ROM, Inc.

Full text CD-ROM disc covers facts and figures for 253 countries worldwide. Illustrations and maps included.

Last Chance to See. *Operating System:* MAC; *Subject:* Reference; *Price:* $39.95; *Grade Level:* JH, HS; *Hardware:* Macintosh, hard drive, 4MB; *Software:* See distributor; *Distributor:* UPDATA.

After years of writing about life on other planets, author and humorist Douglas Adams (*The Hitchhiker's Guide to the Galaxy*) has teamed up with zoologist Mark Carwardine in investigating endangered species on planet Earth. The result is a witty and insightful record of their trip around the world that covered Africa, China, and the South Pacific, among other places. The disc includes hundreds of photographs, narration by Adams, the complete text of his *Last Chance to See* book, and supplementary audio excerpts.

Macademic. *Operating System:* MAC; *Subject:* Reference; *Price:* $79; *Grade Level:* General; *Hardware:* See distributor; *Software:* See distributor; *Distributor:* Bureau of Electronic Publishing.

Includes 7,500 programs and related files for education and instructional use with art, music, math, science, foreign languages, fun and games, teacher's help, and more.

Magazine Article Summaries. *Producer:* EBSCO; *Operating System:* PC; *Subject:* Reference; *Price:* $399 (depending on pkg.); *Grade Level:* General; *Hardware:* IBM compatible 5MB RAM, 40MB hard disk; *Software:* See distributor; *Distributor:* EBSCO.

Covers 370 magazines with abstracts and citations going back as far as 1984.

Monarch Notes. *Operating System:* PC/MAC; *Subject:* Reference/literature; *Price:* $99; *Grade Level:* JH, HS; *Hardware:* See distributor; *Software:* See distributor; *Distributor:* Bureau of Electronic Publishing.

Are you faced with the prospect of a semester's worth of reading in six hours—or just trying to understand the classics? For years, Simon & Schuster's "Monarch Notes" series have been a dream come true for students and parents. And with the release of the CD-ROM edition of the "Monarch Notes," the full text of the entire collection—over 200 different Notes—are available for one low price. No more frantic trips around town searching for the Notes you need, or last minute trips to the library. You can have the entire collection, many of which are no longer in print, for less than 50 cents per Note (single copies can cost $5!).

Multimedia World Fact Book and CIA World Tour. *Operating System:* PC/MAC/MPC; *Subject:* Reference; *Price:* $99; *Grade Level:* JH, HS; *Hardware:* See distributor; *Software:* See distributor; *Distributor:* Bureau of Electronic Publishing.

Whether you're planning a coup in a South American dictatorship or just checking the terrain in Tehran for a tête-à-tête, the CIA has the information you need. Two hundred forty-eight comprehensive country profiles are included.

National Directory. *Operating System:* MAC; *Subject:* Reference; *Price:* $195; *Grade Level:* General; *Hardware:* See distributor; *Software:* See distributor; *Distributor:* Bureau of Electronic Publishing.

A comprehensive listing of the most useful and important addresses, telephone, fax and telex numbers in the United States and the world—120,000 entries. Users can automatically dial or fax numbers, print lists, and export to other programs.

National Register of Historic Places Index on CD. *Producer:* Buckmaster Publishing; *Operating System:* PC; *Subject:* Reference; *Price:*

$295; *Grade Level:* General; *Hardware:* IBM PC or compatible; 640K RAM; CD-ROM player; printer; *Software:* PC-DOS or MS-DOS; Microsoft CD-ROM extensions 2.0 or higher; *Distributor:* EBSCO. Access to over 52,000 places on the U.S. National Register. All U.S. states and territories are included. Each record contains place name, state, country, street address, city, type of place, certification date, criteria indicators, National Historic Landmark Indicator, and reference number. Search results may be printed or saved to disk.

Peterson's Gradline. *Producer:* SilverPlatter Information, Inc. *Operating System:* PC; *Subject:* College/Guidance; *Price:* $695; *Grade Level:* JH, HS, C; *Hardware:* IBM PC or compatible: 640K RAM CD-ROM player; monitor; printer for text; one floppy drive; hard disk recommended; *Software:* PC-DOS or MS-DOS 2.1 or higher, Microsoft CD-ROM extensions; *Distributor:* EBSCO.

A database of 26,000 profiles of 1,400 degree-granting colleges and universities in the United States and Canada offering graduate and professional programs in over 300 academic disciplines. Breakdown to institution, faculty research specialties, degrees conferred, and financial aid.

PhoneDisc Quickref+. *Producer:* Phonedisc USA Corporation; *Operating System:* PC; *Subject:* Reference; *Price:* $317; *Grade Level:* General; *Hardware:* See distributor; *Software:* See distributor; *Distributor:* EBSCO.

One CD-ROM containing three million listings of the most often called corporations, organizations, government agencies, fax, and toll-free numbers in the United States.

PhoneDisc USA (Combination). *Producer:* PhoneDisc USA Corporation; *Operating System:* PC; *Subject:* Telephone Directory; *Price:* $1,868; *Grade Level:* General; *Hardware:* IBM XT, AT, or PS/2 personal computer or compatible; 1MB disk space; 512 internal memory; 5¼" or 3½" floppy drive; Monochrome or color monitor; CD-ROM drive; *Software:* MS-DOS 3.1 or higher, CD-ROM extensions—versions 2.0 or higher; *Distributor:* EBSCO.

PhoneDisc USA is the first personal computer-based telephone directory with listings covering every city in the United States. The entire country is available on only two CD-ROMs that currently contain approximately 90 million names, telephone numbers, addresses, and zip codes. PhoneDisc USA is currently published in two editions, Eastern and Western.

Population Statistics. *Producer:* Slater Hall Information Products; *Operating System:* PC; *Subject:* Reference/Census; *Price:* $1,200; *Grade Level:* General; *Hardware:* IBM PC or compatible; 512K RAM; Standard CD-ROM player; *Software:* MS-DOS 2.1 or higher, Microsoft CD-ROM extensions; *Distributor:* EBSCO.

Detailed 1980 Census data for all places of 10,000 people or more, urbanized areas, metropolitan areas, congressional districts, counties, and states. Also included are the 1986 population and per capita income estimates for approximately 40,000 local areas. Population projections to the year 2000.

Pravda. *Producer:* ALDE Publishing; *Operating System:* PC; *Subject:* Russia; *Price:* $257; *Grade Level:* JH, HS: *Hardware:* IBM PC or compatible; 640K RAM; 10MB hard disk; CD-ROM player; *Software:* PC-DOS or MS-DOS 3.0 or higher, Microsoft CD-ROM extensions; *Distributor:* EBSCO.

A fully indexed database containing a full English translation of Pravda, the vehicle of the Central Committee of the CPSU, for the years 1986 and 1987. Full text of official speeches and announcements offers a critical indicator of Soviet thinking.

Quick Ref+. *Operating System:* PC; *Subject:* Reference; *Price:* $295; *Grade Level:* Elem.–C; *Hardware:* See distributor; *Software:* See distributor; *Distributor:* Bureau of Electronic Publishing.

A single CD-ROM containing 300,000 listings of the most often called corporations, organizations, government agencies, fax and toll-free numbers in the United States. Information can be accessed using a street address, phone number, city, or zip code.

Reference Library. *Operating System:* PC; *Subject:* Reference Materials; *Price:* $130; *Grade Level:* General population; *Hardware:* See distributor; *Software:* See distributor; *Distributor:* UPDATA.

A library of standard reference works: *Webster's New World Dictionary Third College Edition,* with more than 170,000 entries; *Webster's New World Thesaurus,* containing 31,000 entries; *Webster's New World Dictionary of Quotable Definitions; The New York Public Library Desk Reference,* a guide to facts and resources; *Dictionary of 20th Century History; Lasser's Legal and Corporation Forms for the Smaller Business; Webster's New World Guide to Concise Writing; The National Directory of Addresses and Telephone Numbers.*

Street Atlas USA. Operating System: PC; *Subject:* Reference; *Price:* $95; *Grade Level:* General; *Hardware:* IBM/Compatible; *Software:* See distributor; *Distributor:* Bureau of Electronic Publishing.

Detailed, street level maps of every street in the United States (including their names) on one disc. Locations by street name, phone exchange, zip code, or place name. Displays street addresses and city blocks in metropolitan areas. Windows required.

Toolworks MAC. Operating System: MAC; *Subject:* Reference; *Price:* $649; *Grade Level:* General; *Hardware:* See distributor; *Software:* See distributor; *Distributor:* CDiscovery.

Everything you need to get started: Illustrated Encyclopedia, Time Table of History, U.S. History, CD Funhouse.

Toolworks Reference Library. Operating System: PC; *Subject:* Reference; *Price:* $149; *Grade Level:* K–C; *Hardware:* IBM PC; *Software:* See distributor; *Distributor:* CDiscovery.

Includes *The New York Public Library Desk Reference, Webster's New World Thesaurus, Webster's New World Guide to Concise Writing, Webster's New World Dictionary Third College Edition, The Dictionary of 20th Century History, J. K. Lasser's Legal and Corporation Forms for the Smaller Business, Webster's New World Dictionary of Quotable Definitions* and *The National Directory of Addresses and Telephone Numbers.*

TOM Health and Science. Producer: Information Access; *Operating System:* PC/MAC; *Subject:* Reference; *Price:* $1,100 — annual subscription; *Grade Level:* General; *Hardware:* See distributor; *Software:* See distributor; *Distributor:* Information Access.

Provides access to articles from more than 50 publications in the health and science field. Very easy to access information.

Whole Earth Catalog. Operating System: MAC; *Subject:* Reference; *Price:* $149.95; *Grade Level:* General; *Hardware:* See distributor; *Software:* See distributor; *Distributor:* UPDATA.

CD-ROM version of the best-selling *Whole Earth Catalog.* It includes more than 3,500 entries and covers a vast array of subjects — from building your own home to ultralight aircraft and city restoration. Includes a Hypercard feature which allows user to move quickly from subject to subject. Contains more than 700 recordings from bird calls to jazz.

World Almanac and Book of Facts. *Operating System:* PC; *Subject:* Reference; *Price:* $69; *Grade Level:* General; *Hardware:* See distributor; *Software:* See distributor; *Distributor:* CDiscovery.

Categories include more than one million up-to-date facts, area codes, zip codes, and much more.

Zip Plus +. *Operating System:* PC; *Subject:* Reference; *Price:* $195; *Grade Level:* General; *Hardware:* See distributor; *Software:* See distributor; *Distributor:* CDiscovery.

Certified by the U.S. Postal Service, corrects the addresses in a mailing list and inserts the Zip + 4 Zip Codes and carrier route codes.

RELIGION

The Bible Library. *Producer:* Ellis Enterprises; *Operating System:* PC; *Subject:* Bible/Religion; *Price:* $149; *Grade Level:* HS, C, Adult; *Hardware:* IBM PC or compatible; 512K RAM; CD-ROM player; printer for text optional, monitor; *Software:* PC-DOS or MS-DOS, Microsoft CD-ROM extensions; *Distributor:* Bureau of Electronic Publishing.

Nine Bibles and 20 reference works with 31 concordances of Bibles and their references. Strong's numbering system is linked to the original Bible languages. Contains 500 gospel sermons, 500 gospel illustrations, 2,000 miscellaneous short works. Quickly finds all occurrences of Hebrew, Greek, or English words. Five word studies, two dictionaries, two commentaries, and more. Comprehensive religious collection includes over 60 works. Nine complete Bibles: American Standard Version, Literal English Translation, King James Version, New King James Version, Simple English New Testament (four dictionaries and references), Easton's Bible Dictionary, Elwell's Evangelical Dictionary of the Theology, Living Bible, Romanized Hebrew-Greek Bible, New International Version, Revised Standard Version, Edersheim's Life and Times of Jesus the Messiah, Strong's Numbers Linked to Original Hebrew and Greek Words. Six Sermon Outlines and Illustrations (3,000 sermons): 500 Basic Bible Truths, 500 Evangelistic Sermons, 500 Christian Life Sermons, 500 Children's Sermons, 500 Gospel Sermons, 500 Gospel Illustrations. Two Bible Language Dictionaries, three Word Studies, two Commentaries, and 101 Hymn Stories.

King James Bible. *Producer:* Bureau of Electronic Publishing; *Operating System:* PC; *Subject:* Religion; *Price:* $65; *Grade Level:* Elem., JH, HS; *Hardware:* See distributor; *Software:* See distributor; *Distributor:* Bureau of Electronic Publishing.

Search through the entire King James Bible, both the Old and New Testaments, which is completely indexed by words, chapter and verse.

Multi-Bible CD-ROM. Producer: Innotech, Inc.; *Operating System:* PC/MAC; *Subject:* Religion/Reference; *Price:* $130; *Grade Level:* General; *Hardware:* See distributor; *Software:* See distributor; *Distributor:* EBSCO.

This Bible CD-ROM contains a collection of Bible databases including Strong's Numbers, The Revised Standard Version, The New Revised Standard, the King James (authorized) Version, and The New King James Version.

SCIENCE

About Cows. Producer: Quanta Press; *Operating System:* PC/MAC; *Subject:* Science; *Price:* $29; *Grade Level:* General; *Hardware:* IBM PC XT, AT, or compatible; CD-ROM player with card and cable; printer for text (optional); *Software:* PC-DOS or MS-DOS 2.1 or higher, Microsoft CD-ROM extensions; *Distributor:* CDiscovery.

This CD-ROM is a reprint of the Northwood Press volume *About Cows* by Sara Rath. It contains a full text database on one of nature's most wonderful beasts plus black and white and color images of various bovine poses. The disc is for both amateur and serious bovinologists alike.

All About Science. Producer: Intellectual Software; *Operating System:* MAC; *Subject:* Science; *Price:* $395; *Grade Level:* Elem., JH, HS; *Hardware:* See distributor; *Software:* See distributor; *Distributor:* CDiscovery.

Collection of 48 interactive programs that cover all elementary through intermediate science topics in a high-interest format. The programs include: Elementary Science II—electricity, elementary physics, elementary chemistry, elementary biology I & II, behavioral sciences; Investigating our world package—earth and moon system, minerals, rocks, solar system, stars and galaxies, weather and climate, and weather and erosion; Investigating matter and energy package—classifying elements, compounds, heat, how matter changes, magnets and electromagnetism, metric system, MMV electricity, MMV force and motion, physical science, properties of matter, and work and machines; Science of living things package—describing how living things are alike, describing patterns in reproduction, describing the behavior of organisms, discovering how animals stay alive, discovering how plants grow, following genetics from generation to generation, organizing all natural things, organizing animals, organizing plants, organizing protists and fungi, tracing cycle in the environment: ecology, tracking changes through time: evolution, and understanding the human fight to stay healthy, and understanding systems of the human body.

Anatomist. *Operating System:* MAC; *Subject:* Science; *Price:* $295; *Grade Level:* General; *Hardware:* See distributor; *Software:* See distributor; *Distributor:* CD-ROM, Inc.

Based on *The Anatomy Coloring Book* by Harper & Row, this package allows you to move through the body as you learn names, details, and see color images.

Aquatic Sciences and Fisheries Abstracts. *Producer:* Cambridge Scientific Abstracts; *Operating System:* PC; *Subject:* Science; *Price:* $2,495; *Grade Level:* JH, HS, C; *Hardware:* IBM PC or compatible; 640K RAM; standard CD-ROM player; *Software:* PC-DOS or MS-DOS 2.1 or higher; *Distributor:* EBSCO.

A complete international database containing entries drawn from literature supplied by the United Nations Deptartment of International Economic Aid and Social Affairs (FAO), the Intergovernmental Oceanographic Commission (IOC), and leading research centers throughout the world. Included are abstracts and citations from leading journals, as well as reports, serial monographs, dissertations, covering all biological and ecological aspects of marine, freshwater, and brackish environments.

Arctic and Antarctic Regions (1959–Present). *Producer:* National Information Services Corporation; *Operating System:* PC; *Subject:* Science; *Price:* $811; *Grade Level:* General; *Hardware:* IBM PC, XT, AT, PS/2 or compatible; 512 RAM; any CD-ROM drive; monochrome or color monitor; *Software:* PC-DOS or MS-DOS, Microsoft CD-ROM extensions; *Distributor:* EBSCO.

Contains citations compiled by the Science and Technology Division of the U.S. Library of Congress. Five new databases have recently been added: ASTIS, C-CORE, CITATION, SPRILIB, AORIS. All 40 years of the database are indexed on one CD-ROM. The database covers aspects of the life, physical and social sciences, and related engineering, biology, ozone and other matters.

Audubon's Mammals. Operating System: PC/MAC; *Subject:* Science; *Price:* $158 Net; $79 References; *Grade Level:* General; *Hardware:* See distributor; *Software:* See distributor; *Distributor:* CDiscovery.

John James Audubon's 1840 Edition of *Quadrupeds of North America* in full color, text and CD quality sounds from Cornell University's Library of Natural Sounds for many of the mammals.

Biological Abstracts on Compact Disc. *Producer:* SilverPlatter Information; *Operating System:* PC; *Subject:* Science/Biomedical; *Price:* $8,325; *Grade Level:* JH, HS, C; *Hardware:* IBM PC or compatible; 640K RAM floppy or hard disk (hard disk recommended); CD-ROM player; *Software:* PC-DOS or MS-DOS 2.1 or higher, Microsoft CD-ROM extensions; *Distributor:* EBSCO.

The basic research tool for those in the biological and biomedical fields. Entries include bibliographic citations and abstracts of current research reported in biological and biomedical literature. Provides searchable information on author's institutional affiliation, and language information for all citations. There are 250,000 records indexed per year.

Birds of America. *Producer:* CMC ReSearch; *Operating System:* MAC/PC; *Subject:* Wildlife; *Price:* $99; *Grade Level:* JH, HS; *Hardware:* See distributor; *Software:* See distributor; *Distributor:* CDiscovery.

Bird calls can be played through headphones or external speakers. Multi-media disc contains the collection of the first edition plates (500 color VGA images) and text as well as 115 bird call recordings. Audubon describes each bird including its habitat and range. This disc offers high quality color illustrations, CD quality sound, and reference text.

CD-Gene. *Producer:* Software Toolworks; *Operating System:* PC; *Subject:* Science; *Price:* $949; *Grade Level:* HS; *Hardware:* See distributor; *Software:* See distributor; *Distributor:* Bureau of Electronic Publishing.

A genetic sequencing database that contains current versions of four leading DNA and amino acid sequence databases such as GenBank, EMBL and Swiss Prot and Protein Identification Resource.

Cell ebration. *Operating System:* MAC; *Subject:* Science; *Price:* $289; *Grade Level:* Elem.; *Hardware:* See distributor; *Software:* See distributor; *Distributor:* CD-ROM, Inc.

The first program in a new multimedia-based science curriculum for use in grades K–6. Utilizing CD-ROM technology with teacher-directed activities, each of the nine lessons introduces a concept which is then built upon thematically in succeeding lessons. The package contains a teacher's manual, lab equipment and supplies for activities, student science journals, and five multimedia lessons (running over three hours) on CD-ROM. English and Spanish on the same disc.

Chemistry. *Producer:* Queue; *Operating System:* PC; *Subject:* Chemistry; *Price:* $175; *Grade Level:* HC, C; *Hardware:* See distributor; *Software:* See distributor; *Distributor:* CDiscovery.

Four highly rated Chemistry programs from COMPress, Program Design International, Intellectual Software, and Silwa. The titles include: Concepts in General Chemistry – chemical reactions, chemical stoichiometry, ionic equilibrium, mole concept, oxidation-reduction reactions, reaction in aqueous solution; Chemistry Package – elementary chemistry, chemical symbols, general chemistry I & II, chemistry challenge, chemical vocabulary building I, basic inorganic terminology, inorganic nomenclature II and review questions in chemistry; Acid-Base Chemistry – atomic structure, chemical formulas and equation, solutions, physical chemistry, and organic chemistry.

Comprehensive Review in Biology. *Producer:* Queue; *Operating System:* MAC/PC; *Subject:* Study Skills/Guidance; *Price:* $295; *Grade Level:* HS, C; *Hardware:* See distributor; *Software:* See distributor; *Distributor:* CDiscovery.

A compilation of programs that offer extensive reviews and practice in biology. The titles include: Comprehensive Review in Biology Package, Biology I and II, Advanced Placement Biology Test Preparation, CBAT Biology, and SEI Biology.

Darwin. *Operating System:* MAC/PC; *Subject:* Reference, Science; *Price:* $89; *Grade Level:* JH, HS; *Hardware:* See distributor; *Software:* See distributor; *Distributor:* CD-ROM, Inc.

The collected works of Charles Darwin. A guide to teaching about Darwin which can be for all ages.

Down to Earth. *Operating System:* MAC; *Subject:* Science; *Price:* $249; *Grade Level:* General; *Hardware:* Macintosh Plus/SEII/portable 1MB RAM; *Software:* 6.0.0; *Distributor:* UPDATA.

A collection of environmental pictures of foliage, landscape, marine environments, and more.

Drug Information Source — A. Producer: Cambridge Scientific Abstracts; *Operating System:* PC; *Subject:* Reference/Science; *Price:* $2,750; *Grade Level:* JH, HS, C; *Hardware:* IBM PC or compatible; 640K RAM; CD-ROM player; one floppy drive; hard drive; monitor, printer (optional); *Software:* PC-DOS or MS-DOS 3.1 or higher; *Distributor:* EBSCO.

Detailed information on every drug entity available in the United States. Data includes information on concentration, usage, stability, pH dosage administration, compatibility, chemistry, pharmacology, interactions, and toxicity, along with bibliographic citation and drug monographs. This database contains the *International Pharmaceutical Abstracts, AHFS Drug Information,* and *Handbook on Injectable Drugs* all on one disc.

Life Science Collection — Current 1982-1990. Producer: Cambridge Scientific Abstracts; *Operating System:* PC; *Subject:* Science; *Price:* $4,995; *Grade Level:* General; *Hardware:* IBM PC, AT, XT, or compatible; 640K; one floppy and one hard drive CD player; monitor; printer (optional); *Software:* PC-DOS or MS-DOS 3.1 or higher; *Distributor:* EBSCO.

Contains abstracts from more than 5,000 journals, books, conference reports, U.S. patents, statistical publications, and other pertinent English/non-English sources. Authors, titles, subject phrases, key words, source information, and a variety of other fields are available for information retrieval. Conduct searches for specific terms or expand your search into broad subject areas. This disc contains information from current and 1982-90 backfiles.

Life Sciences Collection. All other information is the same as for Life Sciences Collection — Current 1982-1990.

Contains abstracts from more than 5,000 journals, books, conference reports, U.S. patents, statistical publications, and other pertinent English/non-English sources. Authors, titles, subject phrases, key words, source information, and a variety of other fields are available for information retrieval. Conducts searches for specific terms or expands your search into broad subject areas. This disc contains information from current and 1986-90 backfiles.

Life Sciences Collection — Current Disc Plus 2 Years Back. All other information is the same as for Life Sciences Collection — Current 1982-1990.

Mammals: A Multimedia Encyclopedia. Producer: National Geographic; *Operating System:* PC; *Subject:* Science; *Price:* $129; *Grade Level:*

K, Elem., JH; *Hardware:* See distributor; *Software:* See distributor; *Distributor:* Bureau of Electronic Publishing.

An invaluable teaching aid which brings the animal kingdom to life right on the screen. From aardvark to zorilla, it displays photographs and information on each animal. Students can watch animals leap, dive, and fly with this new CD-ROM from National Geographic.

McGraw-Hill Science and Technical Reference Set, 2.0. *Producer:* McGraw-Hill; *Operating System:* PC; *Subject:* Science; *Price:* $495; *Grade Level:* General; *Hardware:* IBM PC, XT, AT or compatible; 640K RAM; CD-ROM player; a hard disk is highly recommended; printer (optional); *Software:* PC-DOS or MS-DOS 2.0 or higher; *Distributor:* EBSCO.

Release 2.0 is greatly enhanced not only by including updated texts from the *McGraw-Hill Concise Encyclopedia of Science and Technology, 2nd Edition* and the *McGraw-Hill Dictionary of Scientific and Technical Terms, 4th Edition* but by improved search and retrieval software. The CD-ROM provides instant access to concise, authoritative, and accurate coverage of 75 major disciplines of science and engineering via full text search or by HyperText "Links" between associated items.

Multi-Media Audubon's Mammals. *Producer:* CMC ReSearch, Inc.; *Operating System:* PC/MAC; *Subject:* Mammals; *Price:* $79; *Grade Level:* JH, HS; *Hardware:* See distributor; *Software:* See distributor; *Distributor:* EBSCO.

John James Audubon's beautiful, classic mammal prints are now available on mûlti-media CD-ROM. The rare and complete 1840 edition of *Quadrupeds of North America* includes plates in full color ($640 \times 480 \times 256$ colors) and the text, as well as CD quality sounds from Cornell University's Library of Natural Sounds for many of the mammals. One of the leading naturalists of his time, Audubon compiled detailed information about each mammal. This disc is a companion to CMC's Multi-Media Birds of America.

Multi-Media Birds of America. *Producer:* CMC ReSearch, Inc.; *Operating System:* PC; *Subject:* Birds; *Price:* $104; *Grade Level:* JH, HS; *Hardware:* IBM PC or compatible; 640K RAM; hard disk with 1MB avaialble; VGA color monitor and card to view graphics; monochrome; *Software:* PC-DOS or MS-DOS, Microsoft CD-ROM extension; *Distributor:* EBSCO.

Includes full color lithographs and text from the original 1840 first edition octavio set of Audubon's *Birds of America* plus "Bird Calls" through the courtesy of Cornell University's Library of Natural Sounds.

The Plant Doctor. Producer: Quanta Press; *Operating System:* PC; *Subject:* Botany; *Price:* $136.50; *Grade Level:* Elem.–C; *Hardware:* IBM PC or compatible; 640K RAM; CD-ROM player; monitor; printer for text; one floppy drive; hard disk recommended; *Software:* PC-DOS or MS-DOS 2.1 or higher, Microsoft CD-ROM extensions; *Distributor:* EBSCO.

Replicates the text and images contained in UWEX printed edition. This is a multi-media disc that allows the user to evaluate, diagnose, and treat unhealthy plants in the "urban" environment. Over 100 plant disorders are included in the database. Major categories include: pesticides, soil, insects, diseases, weeds, vertebrate pests, evergreens, flowers, fruit crops, vegetable crops, shade trees, shrubs and vines, turf.

The Right Images. Operating System: MAC; *Subject:* Science; *Price:* $158; *Grade Level:* K, Elem., JH, HS; *Hardware:* See distributor; *Software:* See distributor; *Distributor:* Bureau of Electronic Publishing.

Includes 103 images covering stars, galaxies, the earth, planets, the moon, shuttle launches, and other spacey topics.

Scenic and Nature III. Operating System: MAC; *Subject:* Photography; *Cost:* $129; *Grade Level:* General; *Hardware:* See distributor; *Software:* See distributor; *Distributor:* Bureau of Electronic Publishing.

On this disc you will find spectacular sunsets, magnificent mountains, fabulous forests, colorful canyons, along with even more of Mother Nature's masterpieces. These photographs can be used for a wide variety of design applications if you only use your imagination.

Science Helper. Operating System: PC; *Subject:* Science; *Price:* $195; *Grade Level:* K–8; *Hardware:* See distributor; *Software:* See distributor; *Distributor:* Bureau of Electronic Publishing.

Over 1,000 science and mathematics lesson plans for kindergarten to eighth grade developed over a 15-year period with an $80 million investment from the National Science Foundation.

Space and Science Sampler. Producer: NASA; *Operating System:* PC; *Subject:* Science; *Price:* $79; *Grade Level:* General; *Hardware:* IBM/Compatible; *Software:* See distributor; *Distributor:* University of Colorado.

Urban Phytonarian. Producer: Bureau of Electronic Publishing; *Operating System:* PC; *Subject:* Science; *Price:* $149; *Grade Level:* Elem., JH, HS: C; *Hardware:* See distributor; *Software:* See distributor; *Distributor:* CDiscovery.

Multimedia database on trees, flowers, shrubs, turf, and flora.

Voyage to the Planets (Volumes 1–7). *Operating System:* PC/MAC; *Subject:* Science; *Price:* $149.95 per volume; *Grade Level:* HS; *Hardware:* See distributor; *Software:* See distributor; *Distributor:* UPDATA.

Volume 1—Uranus, Jupiter, Saturn and the Moons; Volume 2—Neptune; Volume 3—Mars; Volume 4—Venus; Volume 7—the Moon.

Explore the planets without having to leave your computer. Hundreds of Voyager I and II images that enable the user to discover planets of the solar system and their moons. The user can use the included XZoom function to zoom into details of the image with remarkable clarity and can move and manipulate images in the user's own desktop publishing program. Pop-up windows with text describing the image being viewed make this an excellent teaching tool. This product was originally developed for NASA. Twelve special filters were used to create clear images.

Voyage to the Stars, Volume 1: Deep Space Galaxies. *Operating System:* PC/MAC; *Subject:* Science; *Price:* $149.95; *Grade Level:* Elem., JH, HS, C; *Hardware:* See distributor; *Software:* See distributor; *Distributor:* UPDATA.

Images from Mt. Palomar, ESO, Kitt Peak Observatory, and other large telescopes depicting many of the most spectacular galaxies visible from Earth. A bonus is a collection of images of Polar-Ring Galaxies, galaxies which have merged in space by running into each other. These are from the Space Science Telescope Institute, the Bradley Whitmore Collection. Pop-out windows with text describe the image being viewed.

Voyage to the Stars, Volume 2: David Malin Collection. *Operating System:* PC/MAC; *Subject:* Science; *Price:* $149.95; *Grade Level:* General; *Hardware:* 640K RAM, DOS , 3.2 or higher—VGA/SVGA MAC II or better; 2MB RAM; Hard Disk; Color Monitor REC; *Software:* Provision; *Distributor:* UPDATA.

These are astronomical images by David Malin, a renowned astral photographer working with the Anglo-Australian Observatory. These are True-Color Images, using a process that utilizes maximum image fidelity. Pop-out windows with text describing the image make this an excellent teaching tool.

World Weather Disc. *Operating System:* PC; *Subject:* Science; *Price:* $249; *Grade Level:* General; *Hardware:* See distributor; *Software:* See distributor; *Distributor:* Bureau of Electronic Publishing.

Contains a massive meteorological database that describes the climate of the Earth both recently and during the past hundred years. Includes Global Data Sets and U.S. Data Sets.

SPORTS

Baseball's Greatest Hits. *Operating System:* MAC; *Subject:* Sports; *Price:* $59.95; *Grade Level:* Elem., JH, HS; *Hardware:* See distributor; *Software:* See distributor; *Distributor:* CDiscovery.

A collection of historical audio and video of baseball's greatest plays and moments in history.

Sporting News Baseball. *Operating System:* PC/MAC; *Subject:* Major league baseball; *Cost:* $129; *Grade Level:* General; *Hardware:* IBM/ MAC; *Software:* See distributor; *Distributor:* CDiscovery.

Contains a multimedia database of statistics, personalities and details on Major League games.

STORIES

Aesop's Fables. *Operating System:* MAC; *Subject:* Literature; *Price:* $80; *Grade Level:* Elem., JH; *Hardware:* See distributor; *Software:* See distributor; *Distributor:* Ztek.

Ten of the ancient Greek instructive tales in this Discis title. Illustrated with English text. English and Spanish audio.

Amanda Stories. *Operating System:* PC/MAC; *Subject:* Reading/Education; *Price:* $59.95; *Hardware:* See distributor; *Software:* See distributor; *Distributor:* UPDATA.

Ten children's stories feature the hijinks of spunky Inigo the Cat and the clever Your Faithful Camel. Kids point and click, moving through one rolicking adventure after another. Complete interactivity lets children create a new story each time they play. Graphics and varied sounds add to fun. These stories have won several prizes including the Parent's Choice Award and MacWorld's SuperStacks Award.

Annabel's Dream of Ancient Egypt. *Operating System:* PC/MAC; *Subject:* Reading/Music/Egypt; *Price:* $69; *Grade Level:* Elem.; *Hardware:* IBM PC, 640 RAM, DOS, Macintosh; *Distributor:* UPDATA.

An original children's story about a cat who dreams of being a queen. The story is fully illustrated and narrated in stereo CD-Audio with built-in story controls designed to build stronger reading skills. These include a multimedia glossary, spelling, games, and more. Learning topics such as ancient Egypt and opera are introduced in separate modules complete with images, audio, and text. An introduction to Verdi's *Aida* is presented with story and music selections. In addition, there are many hands-on activities like a hieroglyphics translator, a recipe for making paper, an excavation exercise, portrait gallery, and more. Assembled by well-known children's reference author Allan Carpenter and written by Jere Williams.

Children's Favorite Stories, Poems, and Fairy Tales. *Producer:* Queue; *Operating System:* MAC; *Subject:* Literature; *Price:* $95; *Grade Level:* K–4; *Hardware:* See distributor; *Software:* See distributor; *Distributor:* CDiscovery.

Children in grades K–4 will be challenged and entertained by a collection of readings that feature popular stories by famous authors. They include five of the most popular Beatrix Potter animal tales, the classic "Little Red Riding Hood," "Cinderella," "Jack and the Beanstalk," and "The Velveteen Rabbit"; two volumes of popular Mother Goose nursery rhymes, and a collection of children's poems and songs.

Cinderella. *Operating System:* MAC; *Subject:* Literature/Stories; *Price:* $69; *Grade Level:* Elem.; *Hardware:* See distributor; *Software:* See distributor; *Distributor:* CD-ROM, Inc.

Cinderella still marries the prince, but she also finds rooms in the palace for her two stepsisters.

Discis. *Producer:* Discis; *Operating System:* MAC; *Subject:* Reading; *Price:* $750; *Grade Level:* K, Elem.; *Hardware:* See distributor; *Software:* See distributor; *Distributor:* CDiscovery.

Appropriate for kindergarten to grade 6 reading level, the Discis 10-Book library includes books by well-known children's authors, such as: Beatrix Potter, *The Tale of Peter Rabbit* ($85), *The Tale of Benjamin Bunny* ($70); Robert Munsch, *Thomas Snowsuit* ($75), *Mud Puddle* ($75), *The Paper Bag Princess* ($70); *Cinderella,* the original fairy tale ($70); *Scary Poems for Rotten Kids* ($85) by Sean O'Hugin; *A Long Hard Day on the Ranch* ($70) by Audrey Nelson; *Heather Hits Her First Home Run* ($85) by Ted Plantos; and *Moving Gives Me a Stomach Ache* ($85) by Heather McKend. Discis books appear on screen as actual pages of a book with text and illustrations enhanced with voices, music and sound effects. (Discis books can be purchased separately.)

Favorite Folk Tales. *Producer:* Queue; *Operating System:* MAC; *Subject:* Literature; *Price:* $95; *Grade Level:* Elem., JH, HS; *Hardware:* See distributor; *Software:* See distributor; *Distributor:* CDiscovery.

A collection of folk tales from around the globe including stories from North America—Eskimo, Hopi, and African-American tales, Europe, the Far East, and Mexico, plus Paul Bunyan stories, and Rudyard Kipling's *Just So Stories* with sound and music.

Ghost Tracks. *Operating System:* PC; *Subject:* Literature; *Price:* $65; *Grade Level:* JH, HS; *Hardware:* See distributor; *Software:* See distributor; *Distributor:* CD-ROM, Inc.

Five hundred and one classic tales of horror, mystery and the fantastic. One hundred thirty authors including Dickens, Bierce, Poe, Stoker, and Twain. Accompanying illustrations and an oversized print mode for the visually impaired.

Heather Hits Her First Home Run. *Operating System:* MAC; *Subject:* Literature/Stories; *Price:* $84; *Grade Level:* Elem.; *Hardware:* See distributor; *Software:* See distributor; *Distributor:* CD-ROM, Inc.

The pressure is on her to save the game and she goes through many different emotions as she stands at the plate.

Journeys—Emergent Level One. *Operating System:* MAC; *Subject:* Literature; *Price:* $79; *Grade Level:* Ages 3 and up; *Hardware:* See distributor; *Software:* See distributor; *Distributor:* CD-ROM, Inc.

Variety of stories, poems, and songs with illustrations. The collection includes: "Fishing," "I Like Rain," "A House for a Mouse," "Supper for a Troll," "The Horrible Thing with Hairy Feet," and "Stacks of Caps."

Journeys—Emergent Level Two. *Operating System:* MAC; *Subject:* Literature and Stories; *Price:* $79; *Grade Level:* Ages 3 and up; *Hardware:* See distributor; *Software:* See distributor; *Distributor:* CD-ROM, Inc.

Collection includes: "Are You There?," "What Would You Like?," "I'm a Prickly Crab," "Who Will Be My Pet?," "A Most Unusual Pet," "An Animal Alphabet," and "The Tiny Woman's Coat."

Just Grandma and Me. *Operating System:* MAC; *Subject:* Literature; *Price:* $39; *Grade Level:* Ages 3 and up; *Hardware:* See distributor; *Software:* See distributor; *Distributor:* CD-ROM, Inc.

Story which is based on the best-selling book by Mercer Mayer, the award-winning author and illustrator. Little Critter takes a ride on a wind-blown umbrella, fends off a nasty crab, meets a variety of talented starfish and much, much more.

A Long Hard Day on the Ranch. *Operating System:* MAC; *Subject:* Literature/Stories; *Price:* $69; *Grade Level:* Elem.; *Hardware:* See distributor; *Software:* See distributor; *Distributor:* CD-ROM, Inc.

A little boy visits his uncle's farm and the story becomes a tall tale in a letter to his dad.

Mixed-Up Mother Goose. *Operating System:* PC; *Subject:* Literature/reading; *Price:* $59; *Grade Level:* Elem., JH, HS; *Hardware:* See distributor; *Software:* See distributor; *Distributor:* Bureau of Electronic Publishing.

Mixed-Up Mother Goose is the best multimedia game we have ever seen for a PC. It combines animation, fascinating graphics, sound and text with a challenging game, all integrated into a pleasant, interactive story line designed for children four and up. It's so good that children of all ages will enjoy the game — and will be reluctant to leave this fairy land for the real world.

Moving Gives Me a Stomach Ache. *Operating System:* MAC; *Subject:* Literature/Stories; *Price:* $84; *Grade Level:* Elem.; *Hardware:* See distributor; *Software:* See distributor; *Distributor:* CD-ROM, Inc.

The story of a family in the process of moving from the point of view of the little boy.

Mud Puddle. *Operating System:* MAC; *Subject:* Literature/Stories; *Price:* $74; *Grade Level:* Elem.; *Hardware:* See distributor; *Software:* See distributor; *Distributor:* CD-ROM, Inc.

Keeping clean and tidy is a difficult job for any child, especially when a mud puddle is out to get you.

The Night Before Christmas. *Operating System:* MAC; *Subject:* Literature; *Price:* $69; *Grade Level:* K–Elem.; *Hardware:* See distributor; *Software:* See distributor; *Distributor:* CD-ROM, Inc.

This is a classic that both adults and children enjoy. Tale with Arthur Rackham illustrations which keyboard skills are not needed, only the ability to "point and click."

The Paper Bag Princess. *Operating System:* MAC; *Subject:* Literature/Stories; *Price:* $69; *Grade Level:* Elem.; *Hardware:* See distributor; *Software:* See distributor; *Distributor:* CD-ROM, Inc.

A traditional fairy tale with a contemporary twist—the princess is the heroine!

Reading Short Stories. *Producer:* Queue; *Operating System:* PC; *Subject:* Reading; *Price:* $95; *Grade Level:* Elem., JH; *Hardware:* See distributor; *Software:* See distributor; *Distributor:* CDiscovery.

Contains the complete Reading and Interpreting Literature Series from Intellectual Software plus some of the world's greatest short stories and uses them as the basis for interesting, educational tutorials in reading comprehension. The stories, such as *Aesop's Fables, The Emperor's New Clothes, The Ugly Duckling, The Princess and the Pea, The Gift of the Magi, Make Westing, The Tell-Tale Heart, Rumpelstiltskin, Brave Little Tailor,* and *The Lady or the Tiger* are presented with passages that are read at a student's own pace. Then, with the story still on screen, reinforce comprehension as well as critical reading and evaluative thinking skills. Wrong answers result in hints, and, after a second try, feedback is provided in the form of passage which contains the answer.

Scary Poems for Rotten Kids. *Operating System:* MAC; *Subject:* Literature/Poetry; *Price:* $84; *Grade Level:* Elem.; *Hardware:* See distributor; *Software:* See distributor; *Distributor:* CD-ROM, Inc.

Children today live with the same fears we all had as children.

A Silly, Noisy House. *Operating System:* MAC; *Subject:* Reading; *Price:* $59; *Grade Level:* K; *Hardware:* See distributor; *Software:* See distributor; *Distributor:* CDiscovery.

Children explore the rooms of a bright and cheery home, pointing, clicking, and discovering hidden surprises like secret passageways, birthday parties, magic wands and piano-playing spiders! This animated audio toybox also contains over 250 sound effects, songs, and rhymes. Introduces children ages three and over to Macintosh and the world of computers. This disc requires no reading.

The Tale of Benjamin Bunny. *Operating System:* MAC; *Subject:* Literature/Stories; *Price:* $69; *Grade Level:* Elem.; *Hardware:* See distributor; *Software:* See distributor; *Distributor:* CD-ROM, Inc.

Peter Rabbit and his cousin Benjamin Bunny set out to retrieve Peter's clothes.

The Tale of Peter Rabbit. *Operating System:* MAC; *Subject:* Literature/ Stories; *Price:* $84; *Grade Level:* Elem.; *Hardware:* See distributor; *Software:* See distributor; *Distributor:* CD-ROM, Inc.

The story of Peter's escape from Mr. McGregor's garden.

Talking Classic Tales. *Operating System:* PC/MAC; *Subject:* Reading; *Price:* $99; *Grade Level:* P–2; *Hardware:* IBM/Macintosh; *Software:* See distributor; *Distributor:* CDiscovery.

Animation, sound effects and illustrations bring *Puss in Boots, Rumpelstiltskin, The Elves and the Shoemaker, The Queen Bee,* and *The Frog Prince* to life for young readers.

Talking Jungle Safari. *Producer:* New Media School; *Operating System:* PC/MAC; *Subject:* Science; *Price:* $99; *Grade Level:* Elem., JH; *Hardware:* IBM/Macintosh; *Software:* See distributor; *Distributor:* CDiscovery.

Interactive journey into the African jungle with full-color graphics, sound effects, and narration. Take a helicopter, jeep, or riverboat to explore the safari terrain: plains, riverfront, rain forest, and tall grass.

Thomas' Snowsuit. *Operating System:* MAC; *Subject:* Literature/Stories; *Price:* $74; *Grade Level:* Elem.; *Hardware:* See distributor; *Software:* See distributor; *Distributor:* CD-ROM, Inc.

The frustration of adults and children alike during snowsuit weather.

Glossary of Terms

Access Time: A term that can be used to describe several types of activities. (1) The amount of time it takes to get an instruction or a unit of data from computer memory to the processing unit of a computer. (2) The amount of time it takes to get a unit of data from a direct access storage device to computer memory.

Acoustic Modem: A type of modem that uses the handset of an ordinary telephone to transmit signals from the micro computer to the distant computer and back again.

Address: The specific location on a CD-ROM disc where a particular file or piece of information can be found. (1) A coded representation of the destination of data, or their originating terminals. Multiple terminals on one communication line have unique addresses. Messages carry an address before the text to indicate the destination of the message. (2) Either a specific location in the computer memory, a specific location on a direct access storage device, or a relative location.

Algorithm: A method of problem solving by which solutions are derived from a prescribed set of well-defined steps in a finite number. Any step-by-step procedure for arriving at a solution to a specific problem.

Analog: That which is continuously available (often expressed as a wave), as opposed to that which is discretely variable (often expressed as pulses). Analog data often graphically represented as a sine curve. Representation which bears some physical relationship to the original quantity: usually electrical voltage, frequency, resistance, or mechanical translation or rotation.

Analog Monitor: One that displays an unlimited range of brightness for each primary color.

Application Program: One that performs useful work not related to the computer itself.

Application Software: Programs designed to perform a user specific task. Examples of application software include word processing and full-text search and retrieval packages.

Archive: A filing system for information designed to be kept for a long time.

ASCII: (American Standard Code for Information Interchange)— Pronounced "ask-ee," ASCII is the binary transmission code used by most teletypewriters and display terminals. A code established by the American Standards Association in an attempt to standardize data representation in order to achieve compatibility among all data processing systems. Used in computers and communication systems in which each character number or special character is defined in eight bits.

ASCII File: A text file on a machine that uses the ASCII character set.

Autoexec: In MS-DOS (PC-DOS), AUTOEXEC.BAT is the name of the file that contains commands to be executed whenever the computer boots up.

Backup: A copy of any file, disk, or program containing data. The term refers to both user files and application programs.

BAT File: In MS-DOS (PC-DOS), a BAT (batch) file is a file whose name ends in ".BAT," and which contains a list of commands.

Baud: This is the unit of measurement used to indicate the speed with which data is transferred from one device to another by communication systems. The term usually refers to modem-to-modem transmissions and customarily will be the rate of 300, 1200, or 2400 bauds or bps (bits per second).

Bios: Basic input/output system. These are software programs built into the IBM PC's ROM. They make it possible for the CPU to interact with its input/output devices such as the monitor, printer, the disk drives, and the keyboard.

Bit: A bit is a binary (zero and one) digit and the smallest piece of data recognized by the computer. The term is a contraction for binary digit. Data bits are used in combination to form characters; framing bits are used for parity and transmission synchronization.

Board: A printed circuit.

Boolean Search: A search strategy for selected information that uses *and, or,* and *not* functions.

Boot: To start up a computer. May be done as a cold boot, when the computer is initially switched on or as a warm boot, which is used to rest the computer system after it has been in operation.

Buffer: A temporary storage device that is used to compensate for a difference in data flow rates or in time of data flow in events when transmitting data from one device to another.

Bus: The main concentration avenue in a computer. If the computer did not have a bus, it would require separate wires for all possible connections between components.

Byte: The amount of memory space needed to store one character. A byte is normally made up of eight bits.

Cache: A place where data can be stored to avoid having to read the data from a slower device such as a disk.

Catalog: A list of the contents of a disk.

CD/1: Compact disc/interactive. CD/1 is a technical specification proposed jointly by Philips and Sony for a consumer product based on CD-ROM technology.

CD-ROM: Compact Disc-Read Only Memory. This refers to the use of compact discs as a computer storage medium. CDs can store 680 megabytes (MB) of information on a single disc.

CGA: Color/Graphics Adapter. This is a video card for the IBM computer. Software written for the CGA will usually run on the EGA and VGA modes.

Channel: A path or circuit along which information flows.

Character: May be a number, letter, punctuation mark, or other symbol which is uniquely expressed in computer code.

Character String: Any group of characters acted upon in a computer system as though it were a single unit.

Chip: Chips are made of highly refined silicon (sand). Chips may be memory chips or they may be control chips for other types of chips. One type of chip, a PROM, is programmable and cannot be changed. Another type, an EPROM, is programmable but also erasable.

Clip Art: Artwork that can be freely reproduced.

Clock: A circuit that generates a series of evenly spaced pulses.

Clone: A computer that is an exact imitation of another or a software product that exactly imitates another.

Color Graphics: A bit-mapped graphics display adaptor for IBM PC–compatible computers. Displays four colors simultaneously with a resolution of 200 pixels horizontally and 320 pixels vertically or displays one color with resolution of 640 pixels horizontally and 200 vertically.

Color Monitor: A computer display device that displays an image in multiple colors, unlike a monochrome monitor that displays one color on a black or white background.

Company Network: A wide-area computer network, such as DEC ENET (the international engineering network of Digital Equipment Corporation), that often has automatic gateways to cooperative networks such as ARPANET and TELNET for functions such as electronic mail.

Compatible: (1) Two devices are compatible if they can work together. (2) Two computers are said to be compatible if they can run the same programs.

Compression: The reduction or gain of a signal with respect to the reduction or gain at another level of the same signal (see Data Compression).

Computer System: A complete computer installation — including peripherals, such as disk drives, a monitor, and a printer — in which all the components are designed to work with each other.

CONFIG: In MS-DOS (PCC-DOS) the file CONFIG.SYS contains information about the machine configuration, including the type of keyboard and the amount of memory to be set aside for disk buffers.

Configure: To set up a computer or program to be used in a particular way.

Controller: Any hardware or software element or group of elements through which system data are converted during input and output to a peripheral device to affect communications between the system and peripheral.

Conversion: Procedure by which a program recording on one format is transferred to another format, e.g., paper to microform, microform to electronic information.

Coprocessor: A separate circuit inside a computer that adds additional functions to the CPU or handles extra work while the CPU is doing something else.

CPU: The Central Processing Unit is the part of a computer where arithmetic and logical operations are performed and instructions are decoded and executed. The CPU controls the operation of the computer.

Crash: A computer is said to crash when a hardware failure or program error causes the computer to become inoperable.

Cursor: A symbol which indicates the point at which new data may be entered on the computer screen. In the IBM the cursor is a blinking underline.

Daisywheel Printer: Uses a rotating plastic wheel as a type element.

Database: This describes a collection of digitized information that may be manipulated and retrieved by means of a computer.

Debug: To remove errors from a program.

Default: An assumption that a computer makes unless it is given specific instructions to the contrary.

Default Drive: When a microcomputer is operated under MS-DOS, one of the disk drives is designated as the default drive.

Descriptor: In database management, a term used to classify a data record so that all records sharing a common subject can be retrieved as a unit.

Device Drivers: These software programs are needed for any microcomputer to communicate with external devices, such as a CD-ROM drive. They are small programs which have to be written for each device that is connected to the microcomputer.

Digital: A function which operates in discrete steps; digital computers manipulate numbers encoded into binary (on-off) forms, while analog computers sum continuously varying forms; digital communication is the transmission of information using discontinuous, discrete, electrical or electromagnetic signals which change in frequency, polarity, or amplitude.

Digital Audio: The storage of sound and music on a compact disc.

Directory: An area where the names and locations of files are stored.

Disc: A data storage device that contains "read-only" information. The user cannot write on, or add to the information on the disc.

Disk: A computer data storage that not only stores information, but can also be written on and or erased at the user's discretion.

Disk Capacity: The storage capacity of a floppy disk or hard disk, measured in kilobytes (K) or megabytes (MB).

Size	Density	System	Drive	Capacity
3.5"	DD	DOS	standard	720K
3.5"	DD	Mac	standard	800K
3.5"	HD	Mac	SuperDrive	1.4M
3.5"	HD	DOS	high density	1.44M
3.5"	HD	DOS 5	high density	2.88M
5.25"	DD	DOS	standard	360K
5.25"	HD	DOS	high density	1.2M

Disk Drive: A device that enables a computer to read and write data on disks.

Document: A file containing a text or a drawing to be printed.

Documentation: The written description of a computer program.

DOS: Disk Operating System. A name for various operating systems.

Dot-Matrix Printer: This type of printer creates characters on paper by striking an inked ribbon with needle-like hammers. Fully formed characters are made up of the resulting dots.

Download: A process during which data is transferred from one computer or peripheral device to another. Especially refers to down-loading files from a main frame computer or an electronic messaging system.

Dump: To transfer data from one place to another without regard for its significance.

EBCDIC: (Extended Binary Coded Decimal Interchange Code) — An eight-bit code used to represent 256 numbers, letters, and characters in a computer system. Developed by IBM and used primarily by IBM equipment.

EGA: Provides all of the graphic modes of the CGA, as well as additional high-resolution modes and sharper text.

Emulation: Imitation of a computing function by a system not originally designed to perform that function.

End User: The person ultimately intended to use a program or system, as opposed to people involved in developing or marketing.

Enter/Return: A key that begins a command, sending the command to the central processing unit (CPU).

EXE File: In MS-DOS (PC-DOS), OS/2 and VAX/VMS, an EXE file contains a relocatable machine code program and has a name ending with "EXE."

Execute: What the instruction says to do.

External Hard Disk: A hard disk equipped with its own case, cables, and power supply. External hard disks generally cost more than internal hard disks of comparable speed and capacity.

File: A collection of information stored as records.

Floppy Disk: A removable and widely used secondary storage medium that uses a magnetically sensitive flexible disk enclosed in a plastic case.

Gigabyte: One billion bytes.

Graphics: Displays on the screen that are pictorial in nature such as graphs, artwork, charts.

Hard Copy: A printout on paper of computer output.

Hard Disk: A storage medium using rigid aluminum disks coated with iron oxide.

Hardware: Consists of all the physical elements in the computer, such as integrated circuits, wires, terminals.

Hercules Graphics Adapter: Provides all of the functions of the IBM MDA (monochrome display adapter), with the same type monitor, plus a high-resolution graphics mode.

Hypercard: An authoring system which is used to create interactive applications.

Hypermedia: A computer-assisted instructional application such as Hypercard that is capable of adding graphics, sound, video, and synthesized voice to the capabilities of a hypertext system.

IBM PC-Compatible Computer: A personal computer – dubbed a clone by industry analysts – that runs all or almost all the software developed for the IBM Personal Computer (whether in PC, XT, or AT form) and accepts the IBM computer's cards, adapters, and peripheral devices.

Input: The data that is fed into the computer for it to process.

Interactive Videodisc: A computer-assisted instruction (CAI) technology that uses a computer to provide access to up to two hours of video information stored on a videodisc.

Interface: An electronic circuit that governs the connection between two hardware devices and helps them exchange data reliably.

Internal Hard Disk: A hard disk designed to fit within a computer's case and to use the computer's power supply.

ISO 9660: A standard established by the international standards organization for volume and file format of CD-ROM disc.

Joystick: A cursor control device widely used for computer games and some professional applications, such as computer-aided design.

Keyword: A word or operation that the computer can recognize and execute.

Kilobit: One thousand twenty-four bits of information.

Kilobyte: The basic unit of measurement for computer memory equal to one thousand twenty-four bytes.

Language: When used in connection with computers it refers to a special set of instructions by which the computer is programmed to operate or by which data may be manipulated.

Laser Printer: Uses a laser beam to generate an image, then transfers it to paper electronically. They are quiet and faster than printers that mechanically strike the paper.

LED: A type of semiconductor frequently used in microcomputer devices to signal on/off conditions in toggle keys.

Load: To energize data from a disk into the computer's random access memory.

Local Area Network: Connection of computers and peripherals such as printers and modems so that they may share the use of devices and software.

Log Off: The process of terminating a connection with a computer system.

Log On: The process of establishing a connection with, or gaining access to, a computer system.

Macintosh: A family of personal computers introduced by the Apple Computer in 1984 that feature a graphical user interface.

MB: Stands for Megabyte. One megabyte is the equivalent of 1,048,576 bytes (1024 × 1024).

MDA: Monochrome Display Adaptor. It provides very sharp readable text, but no graphics, on a monochrome screen.

Megabyte *see* **MB**

Memory: The location in the computer where data and programs may be stored. Memory may be considered to be internal (ROM) or in memory chips or external, or add-on and contained on floppy or hard disks.

Menu: A list of choices that appears on the screen while a particular program is being executed.

Menu Bar: The graphically highlighted bar that indicates the choice to be used in a menu program.

Microprocessor: (1) An integral piece of hardware, a microchip, which performs the logic functions of a digital computer. (2) It is a piece of hardware that houses the computing parts of a computer on one circuit board or in one set of integrated circuits. The microprocessor does not contain the I/O interfaces and memory unit.

Modems: Acronym for "Modulator/Demodulator." A device generally used to convert digital signals (computer data) to analog signals (sound) for transmission across phone lines. The modem at the other end reverses the process.

Monitor: The screen display device of the microcomputer. Sometimes also called a CRT (Cathode Ray Tube).

Monochrome Display Adaptor: See MDA.

Monochrome Monitor: A monitor that displays one color against a black or white background.

Mouse: A speical kind of peripheral device for CPU data manipulation purposes. It is so called because it is shaped something like a mouse and may have two switches on the top resembling eyes. Some application programs for the IBM use mouse technology although it has become popularized primarily by its installation in the Macintosh computer.

MS-DOS: Microsoft Disk Operating System. An operating system for computers that use the 8086 or 8088 microprocessor.

MS-DOS CD-ROM Extensions: A software program developed by Microsoft that allows CD-ROM discs, which adhere to the High Sierra or ISO 9660 standards, to be accessed as if they were a very large DOS drive. CD-ROM applications which require MS-DOS CD-ROM extensions are generally compatible with a CD-ROM drive. This program is generally supplied with the CD-ROM drive.

Multimedia: The presentation of information on a computer using graphics, sound, animation, and text.

Multi-User System: A computer system that enables more than one person to access programs and data at the same time.

Near Letter Quality: Produces output that resembles the print of a cloth-ribbon typewriter.

Network: A set of computers connected together.

Network Interface Card: An adaptor that enables you to hook a network cable to a microcomputer.

Network Operating System (NOS): The system software of a local area network that integrates the network's hardware components.

Operating System: A special kind of software that operates the computer system. An operating system is the initial program that takes charge and controls all subsequent applications programs (software) that is loaded.

Optical Disk: A high-density storage device that uses lasers to create patterns to represent the information. A CD-ROM disc.

Output: The information that the computer generates as a result of its calculations.

Parallel: The connection of different wires to reach the same destination. This type of connection is faster than serial.

Peripheral: A device connected to a computer.

Pixel: A picture element within the monitor which is made up of single dots of light. They are grouped together to create images or graphics. The higher the resolution of the monitor, the greater the number of pixels it will contain.

Port: A connection between the CPU and another device that provides a means for information to enter or leave the computer.

Power Surge: A large increase in line voltage caused by a power outage.

Professional Workstation: A computer work area which allows the user to utilize the available databases. The stations are tailor-made to provide support and accessibility for the patron.

Prompt: A symbol that appears on-screen informing you that the computer is ready to accept application.

Proprietary File Format: A file format developed by a firm to be used for the storage of data created by its products. A proprietary file format usually is unreadable by other firms' application programs.

Public Domain: A computer program is in the public domain if it is not covered by any kind of copyright.

RAM *see* **Random Access Memory**

Random Access Memory (RAM): The part of storage that is volatile and lost when the computer is turned off. All information in RAM must originally come from an applications program or a file which has been loaded after the computer is turned on.

Read-Only: In DOS, a file whose read-only file attribute has been set so that the file can be viewed but not deleted or modified.

Read-Only Memory (ROM): Semiconducted memory circuits that contain prewritten programs of data. The content of ROM circuits is permanent, while the content of random access memory (RAM) is volatile.

Reboot: To restart a computer, that is, turn it off and then on again or by pressing a special key sequence such as a Ctrl + Alt + Del on MS-DOS computers.

Reset Button: A button, usually mounted on the front panel of the system unit, that enables you to perform a boot if the system has stuck so badly that the reset key doesn't work.

Reset Key: A key combination that, when pressed, restarts the computer. This key combination (Ctrl-Alt-Del on DOS machines) provides an alternative to switching the power off and on.

Resolution: A measure of the sharpness of the images a printer or screen can produce. The higher the resolution, the sharper the image or graphic.

RGB Monitor: A color digital monitor that accepts separate inputs for red, green, and blue, and produces a much sharper image than composite color monitors.

Although the Enhanced Graphics Display uses RGB techniques, RGB monitor is synonymous in IBM PC–compatible computing with the Color Graphics Adapter (CGA) standard.

ROM *see* **Read-Only Memory**

Root Directory: The main directory of a disk, containing files and or subdirectories.

SCSI: Small Computer Systems Interface. A standard bus for connecting devices such as disk drives to computers.

Sector: Data on a CD-ROM disc is stored in sectors of 2,352 bytes. Every sector contains its own error detection and correction coding, and has its own unique address on the disc. Smallest addressable unit of a disc's track.

Seek: To seek is to read back data from a CD-ROM disc in an attempt to find a particular file or piece of information. Because seeking on a CD-ROM is time consuming when compared to magnetic disks, the number of seeks required to find the desired information is an important determinant of overall CD-ROM system performance.

Serial: A single wire connection used to carry data. This is slower than parallel connection.

Server: A machine on a network that provides a particular service to other machines.

Shareware: A software that is copyrighted but can be distributed free of charge to anyone.

Simulation: In education, simulation techniques are enabling schools that cannot afford laboratory equipment to offer students a chance to engage in simulated, on-screen versions of laboratory experiments.

Site License: A software license that allows unlimited copying of a computer program for use by a single organization at a specified site or institution.

Sub Directory: A disk directory that is stored in another directory.

Surge Protector: Absorbs brief bursts of excessive voltage coming in from the AC power line.

System Prompt: In a command-line operating system, the prompt that indicates the operating system's availability for system maintenance tasks such as copying files, formatting disks, and loading programs. In DOS, the system prompt shows the current drive. When you see the prompt C>, for example, drive C is the current drive, and DOS is ready to accept instructions. You can customize the system prompt by using the **Prompt** command. See **Command-Line Operating System.**

Terminal: A device that allows the user to interact with a main computer. The computer terminal is called a "data" terminal or "central communication" terminal.

Track: The track on a CD-ROM disc is actually one continuous, three-mile long spiral, beginning in the center of the disc and spiralling outward.

Tutorial: A form of instruction in which the student is guided step by step through the application of a program to a specific task, such as math problems or finding a periodical. Some application programs come with on-screen tutorials that use computer-based training techniques.

Utilities: Programs that assist in the operations of a computer, but do not do the main work.

VGA: Video Gate Array. The video circuit built into the PS/2 model 50 and higher. It provides high-resolution graphics modes and crisp text as well as emulation of the CGA, EGA, and MDA. Many new CD-ROM programs require VGA capability to access the graphics. A VGA monitor and VGA card must be used in these instances.

Video Card: A plug-in circuit board that enables a computer to display information on a particular type of monitor.

Workstation: (1) An extremely powerful microcomputer typically used for scientific and engineering calculations. (2) A hardware package that includes the CPU plus a variety of peripherals such as hard disk, printer, monitor, etc.

Worm: Write Once, Read Many. This is an optical disk where a computer can save information once, then read that information, but cannot change it. In contrast, with a CD-ROM disc, the computer can only read information that has been provided by the distributor of the disc.

Write Protect: To prevent a floppy disk from accidentally being written over. The process of applying a covering (these are metallic strips that are usually provided in a box of floppy disks) over the notch located on the upper right side of the disk.

Suggested Reading

Library Periodicals

The Bookmark. 1949. Quarterly. Free on exchange to libraries (individuals, $4). Joseph Shubert, ed. New York State Library, Gift and Exchange Library, Albany, NY 12230. Circ: 5,000.

Canadian Journal of Information Science/Revue Canadienne des Sciences de l'Information. Quarterly. Membership (nonmembers, $110 Can.). Ethel Auster, ed. Canadian Association for Information Science, University of Toronto Press, Journals Dept., 5201 Dufferin St., Downsview, Ont. M3H 5T8, Canada.

Canadian Library Journal. 1944. Bi-monthly. Membership (nonmembers in U.S., $45 Can.). Jacqueline Easby, ed. Canadian Library Association, 602-200 Elgin St., Ottawa, Ont. K2P 1L5, Canada.

Cataloging and Classification Quarterly. 1980. Quarterly. $105. Ruth C. Carter, ed. Haworth Press, 10 Alice St., Binghamton, NY 13904-1580.

Catholic Library World. 1929. Bi-monthly. Membership, $45 (nonmembers, $60). Natalie A. Logan, ed. Catholic Library Association, 461 Lancaster Avenue, Haverford, PA 19041.

CD-ROM Librarian. The optical media review for information professionals (formerly: *Optical Information Systems Updata/Library & Information Center Applications*). 10/yr. $79.50. Norman Desmarais, ed. Meckler Publishing, 11 Ferry Lane West, Westport, CT 06880.

CD-ROM Professional (formerly *Laserdisk Professional*). 1988. Bi-monthly. $86. Nancy K. Herther, ed. Pemberton Press, 11 Tannery Lane, Weston, CT 06683. Illus., adv.

Collection Building. 1978. Quarterly. $55. Arthur Curley, ed. Neal-Schuman Publishers, 23 Leonard St., New York, NY 10013.

Collection Management. 1975. Quarterly. $115 (individuals, $45). Peter Gsellantly, ed. Haworth Press, 10 Alice St., Binghamton NY 13905-1580. Circ: 668.

College and Research Libraries. 1939. Bi-monthly. Membership (nonmembers, $35). Gloriana St. Clair, ed. American Library Association, 50 E. Huron St., Chicago, IL 60611-2795. Circ: 13,000.

College and Research Libraries News. 1939. 11/yr. Membership (nonmembers, $10). George M. Eberhart, ed. American Library Association, 50 E. Huron St., Chicago, IL 60611-2795. Circ: 10,500.

Communicator. Irreg. Memberhsip (nonmembers, $10). Helene Mochedlover, ed. The Librarian's Guild, AFSCME local 2626, P.O. Box 71568, Los Angeles, CA 90071.

Computers in Libraries (formerly: *Small Computers in Libraries*). 1981. 11/yr. $72.50. Eric Flower, ed. Meckler Publishing, 11 Ferry Lane West, Westport, CT 06880.

Current Research in Library and Information Science. 1974. Quarterly. $234. Pirkko Elliot, ed. Library Association Publishing, 7 Ridgmont St., London WC1E 7AE, England.

Database: The Magazine of Database Reference and Review. 1978. Bimonthly. $89. Database, 11 Tannery Lane, Weston, CT 06883.

Database Searcher. 1984. Monthly. $89.50. Barbara Quint, ed. Meckler Publishing, 11 Ferry Lane West, Westport, CT 06880.

Document Image Automation. 1981. Bi-monthly. $115. Judith Paris Roth, ed. Meckler Publishing, 11 Ferry Lane West, Westport, CT 06880. Illus., index, adv. Circ: 1,000.

Documents to the People. 1972. Membership (nonmembers, $20). Mary Redmond, ed. ALA/GODORT, Jean Kellough, District Manager, Documents, Sterling C. Evans Library, Texas A&M University, College Station, TX 77843. Circ: 2,000.

Education for Information: The International Review of Education and Training in Library and Information Science. 1983. Quarterly. F1.335. R. F. Guy and J. A. Large, eds. Elsevier Science Publications, B.V., Journals Department, P.O. Box 211, 1000 AE Amsterdam, The Netherlands.

The Electronic Library: The International Journal for Minicomputer, Microcomputer, and Software Applications in Libraries. 1983. Bimonthly. $95. David Raitt, ed. Learned Information, 143 Old Marlton Pike, Medford, NJ 08055.

Emergency Librarian. 1973. 5/yr. $40 prepaid (billed, $45). Ken Haycock, ed. Dyad Services, Subscription Department, P.O. Box C34069, Dept. 284, Seattle, WA 98124-1069. Illus., adv. Circ: 10,000.

The Indexer: Journal of the Society of Indexers and of the Affiliated American and Canadian Societies. 1958. S-A. $25. Hazel K. Bell, ed. Society of Indexers, Journal Subscription Officer, 16 Coleridge Close, Hitchin, Herts SG40QX, England. Circ: 2,000.

Information Development: The International Journal for Librarians, Archivists and Information Specialists. 1985. Quarterly. $117. J. Stephen Parker, ed. Carfax Publishing, P.O. Box 25, Abington, Oxfordshire, OX14 3UE, England. Illus., adv. Circ: 500.

Information Hotline. 1969. 11/yr. $150. Barbara H. Settanni, ed. Science Associates International, 465 West End Ave., New York, NY 10024.

Information Retrieval & Library Automation. 1965. Monthly. $66. Susan W. Johnson, ed. Lomond Publishing, P.O. Box 88, Mt. Airy, MD 21771.

Information Services & Use. 1981. Bi-monthly. fl.328. A. E. Cawkell, ed. Elsevier Science Publishing, 52 Vanderbilt Ave., New York, NY 10017.

Information Technology and Libraries (formerly: *Journal of Library Automation*). 1968. Quarterly. Membership (nonmembers, $40). Thomas W. Leonhardt, ed. American Library Association, 50 E. Huron St., Chicago, IL 60611-2795.

Inspel: International Journal of Special Libraries. Quarterly. DM.48. Gerhard Kruse. Universitatsbibliothek der Technischen, Univ. Berlin, Abt. Publikationen, Strasse des 17 Juni 135, D-1000 Berlin 12, Germany.

Interlending and Document Supply. 1971. Quarterly. $33. David N. Wood, ed. British Library, Sales Unit, Boston Spa, Wetherby, West Yorkshire LS23 7BQ, England.

Library PR Newsd. 1978. Bi-monthly. $26.95. Phil Bradbury, ed. Library Educational Institute, RD 1, P.O. Box 219, New Albany, PA 18833.

The Library Quarterly: A Journal of Investigation and Discussion in the Field of Library Science. 1931. Quarterly. $35 (individuals, $23). Stephen P. Harter, ed. University of Chicago Press, Journals Div., P.O. Box 37005, Chicago, IL 60637.

Library Resources and Technical Services. 1957. Quarterly. Membership (nonmembers, $40). Richard P. Smiraglia, ed. American Library Association, 50 E. Huron St., Chicago, IL 60611-2795.

Library Review. 1927. Bi-monthly. Stuart James and Patricia Coleman, eds. Homes McDougall Bookselling, 30 Clydeholm Rd., Glasgow G14 0BJ, Scotland.

Library Software Review. 1982. Bi-monthly. $115. Jennifer Cargill. Meckler Publishing, 11 Ferry Lane West, Westport, CT 06880.

Library Technology Reports. 1965. Bi-monthly. $185. Howard S. White, ed. American Library Association, 50 E. Huron St., Chicago, IL 60611-2795.

Library Trends. 1952. Quarterly. $60. F. W. Lancaster, ed. University of Illinois Press, Journals Dept., 54 E. Gregory Dr., Champaign, IL 61820.

The Reference Librarian. 1981. S-A. $85 (individuals, $36). Bill Katz, ed. Haworth Press, 10 Alice St., Binghamton, NY 13904-1580.

Reference Services Review. 1972. Quarterly. $65. Ilene F. Rockman, ed. Pierian Press, P.O. Box 1808, Ann Arbor, MI 48106.

Research Strategies. 1983. Quarterly. $40 (individuals, $28). Barbara Wittkopf, ed. Mountainside Publishing, 321 S. Main St., No. 300, Ann Arbor, MI 48104.

RQ. 1960. Quarterly. Membership (nonmembers, $35). Elizabeth Futas, ed. American Library Association, 50 E. Huron St., Chicago, IL 60611-2795.

School Library Journal. 1954. Monthly (except June/July). $63. Lilian N. Gerhardt, ed. Bowker Magazine Group, Subscriptions to: P.O. Box 1978, Marion, OH 43305.

School Library Media Quarterly. 1952. Quarterly. Membership (nonmembers, $40). Barbara Stripling and Judy Pitts, eds. American Library Association, 50 E. Huron St., Chicago, IL 60611-2795.

Science and Technology Libraries. 1980. Quarterly. $105 (individuals, $36). Cynthia A. Steinke, ed. Haword Press, 10 Alice Street, Binghamton, NY 13904-1580.

Special Libraries. 1910. Quarterly. Membership (nonmembers, $48). Special Libraries Association, Circulation Department, 1700 18th Street N.W., Washington, D.C. 20009.

Special Libraries Association. Geography and Map Division. Bulletin. 1947. Quarterly. $25. Joanne M. Perry, ed. Special Libraries Association. Subscriptions to: A. Sprankle, 406 E. Smith St., Topton, PA 19562-1121.

Technical Services Quarterly. 1983. Quarterly. $95 (individuals, $36). Gary M. Pitkin, ed. Haworth Press, 10 Alice St., Binghamton, NY 13904-1580.

Technicalities. 1980. Monthly. $42. Brian Alley, ed. Westport Publishers, Media Periodicals Division, 2440 O St., Suite 202, Lincoln, NE 68510.

CD-ROM Journal Listings

Advanced Information Report

publisher:	Elsevier Advanced Technology
frequency:	Monthly
order no.:	014-775-837
price:	$263

BASES

publisher:	FLA Consultants
frequency:	Monthly
order no.:	107-832-677
price:	$220; all others $205

CALICO Journal

publisher:	CALICO
frequency:	Quarterly (Sept. Dec., Mar., June)
order no.:	165-797-853
price:	$35 individual; $65 institution; $125 corporation

Canadian CD-ROM News

publisher:	Canadian Library Association CD-ROM Interest Group
frequency:	Quarterly
order no.:	174-053-207
price:	$24

CD Computing News

publisher:	Worldwide Videotex
frequency:	Monthly
order no.:	188-206-007
price:	$150 N. America; $165 elsewhere

CD Data Report

publisher:	Helgerson Associations, Inc.
frequency:	Monthly
order no.:	188-206-148
price:	$395 U.S.; $495 elsewhere

CD-ROM

publisher:	Worldwide Videotex
frequency:	18 issues
order no.:	188-213-391
price:	1,980 French francs

CD-ROM Databases

publisher:	Worldwide Videotex
frequency:	12 issues
order no.:	188-213-755
price:	$150 U.S. and Canada; $165 elsewhere

CD-ROM Directory

publisher:	Task Force pro Libra
frequency:	Annual
order no.:	188-213-821
price:	£59.20

CD-ROM International

publisher:	A Jour
frequency:	18 issues
order no.:	188-213-946
price:	2,100 French francs

CD-ROM Librarian

publisher:	Meckler Ltd.
frequency:	11 issues
order no.:	188-213-987
price:	£63 in U.K.
order no:	188-213-979
price:	$35 grammar, junior/senior high school libraries in U.S.; $85 all others in U.S.

CD-ROM Market Place

publisher:	Meckler Corporation
frequency:	Annual
order no.:	188-214-027
price:	$30 in U.S.

CD-ROM Professional

publisher:	Pemberton Press Inc. – Online, Inc.
frequency:	Bimonthly
order no:	188-214-274
price:	$86 U.S.; $121 elsewhere

CD-ROMs in Print

publisher:	Meckler Corporation
frequency:	Annual
order no:	188-232-490
price:	$49.50 U.S.

Cogito

publisher:	Verlag Hoppenstedt & Co.
frequency:	Quarterly
order no.:	216-219-733
price:	$48

Document Image Automation

publisher:	Meckler Corporation
frequency:	Quarterly
order no:	279-492-730
price:	£85 except the Americas
order no.:	279-492-722
price:	$35 grammar, junior high and high school libraries; $47 Canada, Mexico, Central/South America grammar, junior high and high school libraries; $115 U.S. all others; $127 Canada, Mexico, Central/South America all others

Document Image Automation Update

publisher:	Meckler Ltd.
frequency:	11 months
order no:	279-492-755
price:	£192 except the Americas
order no:	279-492-748
price:	$297 in the U.S.; $315 Canada/New Mexico

Electronic Publishing

publisher:	John Wiley & Sons
frequency:	Quarterly
order no.:	301-097-101
price:	$185

The Electronic Library

publisher:	Learned Information Ltd.
frequency:	Bimonthly
order no.:	300-852-100
price:	£75 all except North America
order no.:	300-852-092
price:	$95 in North America

Euro-Documentation

publisher:	Admark Publishing Ltd.
frequency:	Monthly
order no.:	317-241-594
price:	£100 Western Europe; £135 elsewhere

IDP Report

publisher:	Knowledge Industry Publications
frequency:	Semi-monthly
order no.:	409-644-507
price:	$349 U.S.

IMC Journal

publisher:	International Information Management Congress
frequency:	6 issues
order no.:	413-015-009
price:	$90; $115 airmail

Imaging Service Bureau News

publisher:	Image Publishing
frequency:	6 issues
order no.:	412-907-628
price:	$120

Imaging Technology Report

publisher:	Microfilm Publishing, Inc.
frequency:	Monthly

order no.:   412-908-519
price: $145 U.S. & Canada

Information Market

publisher: Commission of the European Communities
frequency   5 issues
order no.:   407-022-581
price: Free

Information Today

publisher: Learned Information Ltd. Congress
frequency: Monthly (11 per year, July/August combined)
order no.:   428-764-872
price: £40 (1 year) all except North America

order no: 428-764-864
price: $34.95 (1 year) in North America

Information World Review

publisher: Learned Information Ltd.
frequency: Monthly
order no.:   428-804-355
price: £32 all except North America

order no: 428-804-363
price: $59 in North America

Infotecture — Europe

publisher: Transtez International — A Jour
frequency: 22 issues
order no.:   429-367-816
price: 2,500 French francs

Infotecture — France

publisher: A Jour
frequency: 22 issues
order no.:   429-367-808
price: 2,500 French francs

Inside IT

publisher: John Barker
frequency: 10 issues (approximately)

order no.:   431-160-423
price: £150 (£75 to educational institutions)

Interactive Healthcare Newsletter
publisher: Stewart Publishing, Inc.
frequency: Monthly
order no.:   435-106-059
price: $70 (free MDRVC) additional subscriptions $25 each

The International CD-ROM Report
publisher: Innotech Inc.
frequency: Monthly
order no.:   438-620-353
price: $72

Library Hi Tech
publisher: Pierian Press
frequency: Quarterly
order no.:   524-742-319
price: $65

Library Hi Tech News
publisher: Pierian Press
frequency: 10 issues
order no.:   524-744-513
price: $95 U.S. plus $16 elsewhere

Library Technology Reports
publisher: American Library Association
frequency: Bi-monthly
order no.:   525-388-005
price: $185 U.S. and Canada

Bibliography

Access Faxon. Westbrook, MA: Faxon Press, 1989.

AIIM Buying Guide: The Official Registry of Information and Image Management Products and Services. Silver Spring, MD: AIIM, 1985.

Arms, Caroline. "Using the National Networks: BITNET and the Internet." *Online* (September 1990) pp. 24–29.

Armstrong, C. J., and J. A. Large. *CD-ROM Information Products: An Evaluative Guide and Directory.* Brookfield, VT: Gower Publishing, 1990. 500 pp. Hardcover, $84.95.

Babits, Ann. *CD-ROM Librarian Index: 1986–1990.* Westport, CT: Meckler Publishing, 1991.

Bailey, Charles W. "Electronic (Online) Publishing in Action . . . The Public-Access Computer Systems Review and Other Electronic Serials." *Online* (January 1991), pp. 25–28.

Brandt, Richard. *Videodisc Training: A Cost Analysis.* VA: Videodisc Monitor, 1989.

The CD-ROM Directory. England: TFPL Publishing, 1989.

CD-ROM Market Place, 1991: An International Directory. Westport, CT: Meckler Publishing, 1991.

CD-ROM Yearbook. Bellevue, WA: Microsoft Press, 1989.

CD-ROMs in Print. Westport, CT: Meckler Publishing, 1989.

Compact Optical Disc Technology—CD ROM, April 1979–1986: Citations from the INSPEC Database. Springfield, VA: National Technical Information Service, 1986. PB87-852885/XAB.

Costigan, Dan. *Laser-Optical Storage: The New Dimension in Information Automation.* Bethesda, MD: Avedon Associates, 1988.

Desmarais, Norman, ed. *CD-ROMs in Print, 1992.* Westport, CT: Meckler Publishing, 1991. 550 pp. ISBN 9-88736-780-1. Softcover, $59.50.

————. *CD-ROM Local Area Networks: A User's Guide.* Westport, CT: Meckler Publishing, 1991.

————. *CD-ROM Reviews. 1987–1990: Optical Product Reviews from CD-ROM Librarian.* Westport, CT: Meckler Publishing, 1991.

————. *The Librarian's CD-ROM Handbook.* Westport, CT: Meckler Publishing, 1989. 174 pp. ISBN 0-88736-331-8. Hardcover, $35.

Ditlea, Steve. "HyperTed." *PC/Computing* (October 1990), pp. 201–210.

Drummond, Louis. "Going Beyond Online." *Online* (September 1990), pp. 6–8.

Duggan, Mary K. *CD-ROM in the Library: Today and Tomorrow.* New York: G. K. Hall, 1990.

————. "Copyright of Electronic Information: Issues and Questions." *Online* (May 1991) pp. 20–26.

Educational Videodisc Directory. Washington, DC: Systems Impact, 1989.

Elshami, Ahmed M. *CD-ROM Technology for Information Managers.* Chicago, IL: American Library Association, 1990. 280 pp. ISBN 0-8389-0523-4. Softcover, $35.

Engle, Mary. "Summary of PACS-L Readers Response Concerning Designing Systems to Support Reading Electronic Books." BITNET communication, February 12, 1991.

Ensor, Pat. *CD-ROM Research Collections.* Westport, CT: Meckler Publishing, 1991.

————, and Steve Hardin. *CD-ROM Periodical Index.* Westport, CT: Meckler Publishing, 1991.

Feldman, Tony. *The Publisher's Guide to CD-ROM.* New York: Van Nostrand Reinhold, 1991.

Fox, David. *The CD-ROM Market in Canadian Libraries.* Westport, CT: Meckler Publishing, 1990.

Freeman, Craig C., and Eileen K. Schofied. *Roadside Wildflowers of the Southern Great Plains.* Kansas: University of Kansas Press, 1991.

Gale, John. *State of the CD-ROM Industry: Applications, Players, and Products.* Alexandria, VA: Information Workstation Group, 1987.

————, Clifford Lynch, and Edward Brownrigg. *Report on CD-ROM Search Software.* Alexandria, VA: Information Workstation Group, 1987.

Garrett, John R. "Text to Screen Revisited: Copyright in the Electronic Age." *Online* (March 1991), pp. 22–24.

Guide to Producing Videodiscs in NTSC and PAL. DE: Philips and Du-Pont Optical Company, 1989.

Hane, Paula. "Paper: The Security Blanket of the Electronic Age." *Database* (February 1991), pp. 6–7.

Hart, Michael. "Information About Project Gutenberg." BITNET communication, May 11, 1990.

————. "Project Gutenberg: Access to Electronic Texts." *Database* (December 1990), pp. 6–9.

Helgerson, Linda W. *CD-ROM: Electronic Publishing in Business and Industry.* New York: Van Nostrand Reinhold, 1991.

Helgerson, Linda, and Martin Ennis. *The CD-ROM Sourcedisc.* Alexandria, VA: Diversified Data Resources, Inc., 1987.

Hendley, Tony. *CD-ROM and Optical Publishing Systems.* Westport, CT: Meckler Publishing, 1987.

Hollander, Robert. "Brief Description of Project." BITNET communication, February 21, 1991.

Information and Image Management: The State of the Industry 1989. Silver Spring, MD: AIIM, 1989.

Interactive Videodiscs for Education. Lexington, KY: Ztek Co., 1989.

Isailovic, Jordan. *Videodisc Systems: Theory and Applications.* Englewood Cliffs, NJ: Prentice Hall, 1987.

Lambert, Steve, and Suzanne Ropiequet, eds. *The New Papyrus, CD-ROM.* Bellevue, WA: Microsoft Press, 1986.

McQueen, Judy, and Richard W. Boss. *Videodisk and Optical Digital Disk Technologies and Their Applications in Libraries, 1986 Update.* Chicago: American Library Association, 1986. (This is an update of the Council on Library Resources volume cited above.)

Maracaccio, Kathleen Young. *Computer-Readable Databases: A Directory and Data Sourcebook.* Detroit, MI: Gale Research, 1989.

Micrographic and Optical Recording Buyers Guide. England: Spectrum Publishing, 1989.

Nelson, Nancy Melin. *Library Applications of Optical Disk and CD-ROM Technology.* Westport, CT: Meckler Publishing, 1987.

————, and Meta Nissley. *CD-ROM Licensing and Copyright Issues for Libraries.* Westport, CT: Meckler Publishing, 1990.

Nicholls, Paul. *CD-ROM Collection Builder's Toolkit.* Weston, CT: Pemberton Press, 1990. 210 pp. ISBN 9-10965-01-3. Softcover, $29.95.

1988 Medicaldisc Directory. Alexandria, VA: Paul R. Stewart Publishing, 1988.

Nissley, Meta and Nancy Melin Nelson, eds. *CD-ROM Licensing and Copyright Issues for Libraries.* Westport, CT: Meckler Publishing, 1991. 95 pp. ISBN 0-88736-701-1. Hardcover, $34.95.

Optical Memory Data Storage, 1975–February 1986: Citations from the INSPEC Database. Springfield, VA: National Technical Information Service, 1986. PB86-858248/XAB.

Optical Storage Technology 1987: A State of the Art Review. Westport, CT: Meckler Publishing, 1987.

Rechel, Michael W. "Laser Disc Technology: A Selective Introductory Bibliography." *CD-ROM Librarian* 2 (4) (July/August 1987): pp. 16–24.

Ropiequet, Suzanne, ed. *CD-ROM 2: Optical Publishing*. Bellevue, WA: Microsoft Press, 1987.

Saffady, William. *Optical Disks for Data and Document Storage*. Westport, CT: Meckler Publishing, 1986.

Sherman, Chris, ed. *The CD-ROM Handbook*. New York, NY: McGraw Hill, 1988. 510 pp. ISBN 0-07-0565678-3. Hardcover, $59.95.

Steele, Ken. "Shakespeare Electronic Conference Update." BITNET communication, November 21, 1990.

Timbers, Jill G. "Laserdisc Technology: A Review of the Literature on Videodisc and Optical Disc Technology, 1983–mid-1985." *Library Hi Tech Bibliography 1* (1986): pp. 57–66.

Videodisc and Optical Digital Disk Technologies and Their Applications in Libraries. Washington, DC: Council on Library Resources.

Videodiscs, Compact Disks and Digital Optical Disk Systems. Medford, NJ: Learned Information, 1986.

Index